Praise for *The Trampoline*

"This ground-breaking book is for everyone working in social and public interest services. *The Trampoline Effect* captures the essence of services as caring for others, and bravely addresses critical service tensions between the push for efficiency of systems and the need to recognize people with affection and respect as full individuals. Sarah Schulman and Gord Tulloch share the insider stories and deep engagements that inform their invaluable insights on how systems need to change to become more human. This is a book to be read, shared, and taught."

LARA DE SOUSA PENIN co-founder, Parsons DESIS Lab, and author of *Designing the Invisible*

"*The Trampoline Effect* is a deeply authentic, contextualized, inspiring, and pragmatic guide to reorienting social systems toward human flourishing. In their ambitious collaboration to humanize Canada's disability system, Gord Tulloch and Sarah Schulman do not offer silver-bullet solutions. They offer something better: possibilities."

ALEX RYAN senior vice president, partner solutions, MaRS Discovery District

"In their excellent book, Gord Tulloch and Sarah Schulman offer a new way of thinking about needs, fulfillment, and community involvement. By distilling their insights from deep front-line social service experience into twelve accessible 'stretches' that can be used by anyone who is working to meet community needs, the authors give hopeful aspirations a very practical place to start."

TIM DRAIMIN senior advisor, McConnell Foundation

"Standing out from a sea of statistics in the social services, *The Trampoline Effect* tells a story that is both honest and hopeful. Part field guide and part reflection, it offers insight from the authors' own innovation journey, illuminating not only the need for purpose and healing in those who experience social stigma, but also the same need in each of us. This book points to a new frontier of social services that is capable not only of keeping people safe, but also of feeding people's souls. Along the way, it challenges the long-established beliefs both in social services and in the field of innovation."

DARCY RIDDELL BC program director, MakeWay

"*The Trampoline Effect* is finely spun strategic gold forged in the red-hot heat of deep practical experience on the ground. Reading this book will make you wiser."

ZAID HASSAN co-founder, Reos Partners, and author of *The Social Labs Revolution*

"This is a book for the strong of heart. Gord Tulloch and Sarah Schulman have offered a candid appraisal of the limitations of the service delivery system, and an instruction manual for reconciling that reality through a courageous commitment to justice, equity, accessibility, and inclusion. *The Trampoline Effect* is for policy makers, funders, anyone involved with the service delivery system, and those who understand that taking care of each other is the essence of democracy. With humility, the authors show us that we can do better—we must do better."

AL ETMANSKI & VICKIE CAMMACK co-founders, PLAN; Members of the Order of Canada; and authors

"*The Trampoline Effect* is a wonderful combination of evidence, humility, and everyday alternatives to how we practice the human services. This is not a book that tells us what we are doing wrong; rather, it asks us to stretch ourselves and our practice, to strive for more than safety, security, and conformity with norms and regulations. Honest in both the successes and the failures of their years of real-world experimentation, Sarah Schulman and Gord Tulloch offer us a new way of thinking about what we do, and practical suggestions on how to do it better."

TIM STAINTON director, Canadian Institute for Inclusion and Citizenship

"In our well-meaning efforts to provide for people's material needs, such as food, shelter, and clothing, we've inadvertently diminished their agency, control, and connectedness—the very things that make us human. In *The Trampoline Effect*, Gord Tulloch and Sarah Schulman provide a coherent and compelling alternative vision for our 'human' services, one still rooted in natural empathy but now focused on connecting people to their hopes, stories, capabilities, and relationships. They lay out an elegantly simple— albeit still difficult—grassroots way of getting there. If you want to contribute to the renewal of the social sector, you had better read this book."

MARK CABAJ president, Here to There

"*The Trampoline Effect* is a hugely personal book, deeply grounded in professional experience and pursuing the bold ambition of making social systems more human. It puts the reader into the lived experience of the people social services seek to help, and demonstrates convincingly why current theory and practice is failing. By suggesting twelve thought-provoking 'stretches,' Gord Tulloch and Sarah Schulman invite us to embrace the tensions inherent in the system, rather than shy away from them. The result is a major contribution to social work and the emerging field of social design."

CHRISTIAN BASON CEO, Danish Design Centre, and author of *Leading Public Design: Discovering Human-Centred Governance*

"This book is about far more than disability supports. Rather, it is about all the ways all of us are othered and disempowered: how it came to happen, how it continues, and what we can do about it if we are brave and humble as people, leaders, and organizations. Through a beautifully woven blanket of storytelling and data, *The Trampoline Effect* tells the journey of change-making initiatives, the people involved in them, and the authors themselves as they rise to greet old challenges in new ways. I am sharing this book with the organizations I support, the schools I am working with, my students, my friends with disabilities, and my family—I want it to generate new conversations everywhere I go."

AARON JOHANNES faculty member, Department of Child, Family and Community Studies, Douglas College

"With *The Trampoline Effect*, Gord Tulloch and Sarah Schulman show us that, to get where we need to be, we have to start by deconstructing the equipment we used to build the very idea of *the other*—whether that idea is hidden in our interpersonal relationships, our structures, our ethical postures, our practices, or our policies. Rarely have I come across the perseverance, thoroughness, and intellectual honesty I witness as these authors iterate, dissect, analyze, convey, explore, hijack, dismantle, and weave new avenues to shape a world that has meaning only through the prism of equality."

NADIA DUGUAY co-founder, Exeko, and CKX Fellow

THE
TRAMPOLINE
EFFECT

Redesigning Our
Social Safety Nets

THE
TRAMPOLINE
EFFECT

Gord Tulloch & Sarah Schulman

**REACH
PRESS**

ISBN 978-1-7773148-0-4 (paperback)
ISBN 978-1-7773148-1-1 (ebook)

Published by Reach Press
trampoline-effect.ca

Produced by Page Two
www.pagetwo.com

Edited by Frances Peck
Copyedited by Melissa Edwards
Proofread by Alison Strobel
Cover design by Jennifer Lum
Interior design by Taysia Louie and Fiona Lee
Interior illustrations by Michelle Clement

trampoline-effect.ca

To partners and partnerships

Contents

Preface *1*

Introduction: Stories and experiments *7*

PART I **Beginnings, Undertakings, and Take-Aways** *33*

1 Loosening the flotilla *37*

2 The rise of the professional *41*

3 How the flotilla got stuck *45*

4 Institutions, old and new *49*

5 Living and dying systems *55*

6 Stretching or innovating? *57*

7 No change without examining values *61*

PART II **Three Phases of Experiments** *67*

    8   Phase One: Projects, pilots, and prototypes *71*

    9   Phase Two: Building organizational
       capacity for R&D *85*

   10   Phase Three: Building an R&D culture
       inside organizations *95*

   11   Recovering tensions *109*

PART III **Twelve Stretches** *113*

   12   Stretching our focuses *117*

   13   Stretching our roles *135*

   14   Stretching our frameworks *149*

       Conclusion *171*

       Acknowledgements *175*

       Plain language summary *179*

       Stretch questions *181*

Worthlessness is a drug
And it doesn't even
Cost anything

JANET ROGERS

Preface

SIX HUNDRED AND TWO. An unprecedented number, the policy documents said. The height of the crisis, the politicians lamented. No longer was homelessness hidden in the shelters and back alleys of Surrey, British Columbia. Six hundred and two people in the city were homeless. Two hundred were sleeping outside.

By the time David found himself becoming a 2017 statistic, subsisting in a makeshift tent on 135A Street in Surrey, he had lost everything: his wife, two kids, suburban home, truck, and construction business. When social workers dropped by to offer help, he turned them down. He didn't want a hot meal. He didn't want a shower. He didn't want to sign up for the new portable housing units. Accepting care would mean he was worth something. And he didn't believe that. He didn't believe he deserved much of anything.

The workers who came by offered David the tools for survival: food, shelter, clean needles. But they offered no answers to David's most pressing question: why survive? Other than the attention of the church volunteers, with their free Bibles and compassion, there was little to satisfy his hunger for respect, redemption, hope, and self-overcoming.

Without attention to his deeper needs, David continued downhill. He would overdose, only to be saved, only to overdose again. Dependent on emergency medical services to live, he was trapped in a shame spiral. The shame showed up in his resigned posture. The shame showed up in the near whisper of his voice. The shame showed up in his determination to obliterate the pain.

If we are part of the social sector—whether we're policy makers, organizational leaders, front-line staff, volunteers, or philanthropists—we struggle with how to respond to the human needs before us. We make sandwiches. We run donation drives. We open emergency shelters. We approve stopgap dollars. We do what we can to reduce harm and suffering. But what do we do to increase collective healing and purpose? Until we make it possible for people like David to recover some sense of worthiness and trust, what will really change?

FACED WITH RISING demand, the social sector sees little choice other than to expand. The focus is on more service: more beds, more meals, more safe injection sites, more staff, more coordination between staff. But more service also comes with more people in one place, tighter rules, clearer protocols, and beefed-up security. Moving lots of people through a soup kitchen, for example, requires administrative precision: queue management, standardized food, and armies of volunteers outfitted in hairnets and gloves.

All of these seemingly sensible interactions have unmeasured consequences: solidifying people's stigma and shame, reducing their autonomy and agency, and reinforcing their negative sense of themselves. It's hard not to see yourself as flawed and deficient when in the company of what David called the "parade of lost souls." And yet more resources are rarely enough resources. Social services and their systems are seemingly always cash-strapped. "Can you get the costs down?" and "What's the bare minimum you need?" are constant refrains. Short-term thinking about costs may behoove short-term service contracts and political cycles, but it locks services and systems into a triage trap, one that constantly pits immediate needs for food and shelter against deeper needs for meaning and purpose.

If we fail to see that people's immediate needs and their deeper needs are inextricably linked, and if we in fact service people's physiological needs in ways that deplete their existential needs, we will

The question that is rarely asked, and that cannot readily be answered, is "What is the cost of *not* doing things differently?"

never escape the cycle of more demand, more supply, and still more demand.

The question that is rarely asked, and that cannot readily be answered, is "What is the cost of *not* doing things differently?" What is the system cost of not attending to the hearts, souls, and minds of the Davids we serve? What is the human cost of allowing shame and stagnation to spread? What is the moral and spiritual cost of failing to nourish the languishing soul, the soul that is bereft of hope and meaning, that is unstimulated or directionless?

OVER AND OVER again, in the decades we've worked in the social services, we have seen how prioritizing immediate needs over deeper ones can steadily erode people's potential. Indeed, the very interventions that seek to do good may inadvertently do harm.

Addressing people's need for love, connection, esteem, and self-realization may seem secondary to answering their need for safety and stability. But these are all concurrent needs. If people like David don't believe in themselves and in the future, they will keep slipping through the cracks, immune to offers of help, caught in an expensive decline.

Our political, policy, and procurement systems see the numbers of people in need, but they are distanced from the stories of who and what make up those needs. Staff on the ground cannot and should not keep their distance. To parse out needs alone is to reduce people to widgets.

And so we come to the crux of the matter, and the reason for this book: learning how to make our social systems more human.

There exists, in the social sector, a fierce tension between system mandates and personal duties. The first is about supplying efficient and basic levels of care; the second is about empathy and love. The first is about taking care of others; the second is about caring for others. If we tamp down the feelings and obligations that come from our personal relatedness to others, if we train employees to see themselves as mere vessels delivering system mandates, we risk putting ourselves in a position that is morally unsustainable. And we risk existential harm to others.

Wouldn't it be better, both morally and pragmatically, for all of us in the social sector to figure out how to harness our natural interest in the well-being of others so that it enriches the people and systems we serve? Wouldn't it be better to acknowledge the many tensions that strain how we care, and rather than ameliorate those tensions with more rules and structures, engage with them and, in doing so, stretch into fresh mindsets and practices?

This book is about how we might offer the Davids of the world not just a life but a flourishing life. It's about pushing our systems to reach from the lowest common denominator to the highest: from safety and stability to growth and actualization. What's needed to stimulate growth and actualization is profoundly different from what's needed to secure safety and stability. What's needed is nothing less than a reimagination of what we do.

Nothing has given me more hope recently than to observe how simple conversations give birth to actions that can change lives and restore our faith in the future. There is no more powerful way to initiate significant social change than to start a conversation. When a group of people discover that they share a common concern, that's when the process of change begins.

MARGARET J. WHEATLEY

Stories and experiments

Gord's story

I N 1991 I responded to a newspaper ad to work with people with intellectual disabilities. I had just arrived in Vancouver and was working part-time as a bartender and a philosophy instructor, and I needed more work. I thought picking up some casual shifts might round out my employment experience and keep things real, so to speak.

John was the first person with an intellectual disability that I ever worked with. I was nervous when I showed up for my orientation and knocked on the front door of his bungalow home. The supervisor answered it, introduced himself, and then called to John to come meet me.

John strolled around the hall corner, crossed the living room, and came to within a few feet of me, all without saying a word. He was six-foot-three, 275 pounds, and bald—an imposing figure. The scowl made things worse. He gave me the once-over, head to toe and back, and exclaimed "Bigfoot!" Then he laughed, turned around, and went back to his room. And that was my name thereafter. Actually, it was Bigfoot when he wanted to poke fun, Ghost for the everyday.

In the orientation that day the supervisor informed me that John "lies a lot." There was a protocol in place for when this happened:

whenever John started to tell an untrue story, I was supposed to inter-rupt and ask him if it really happened. If it hadn't happened, I was to ask him to say only things that were true.

I might have done that once or twice in the first week, but then I stopped. The rule felt wrong. It made me very uncomfortable. John's stories, as fantastical as they were, were not lies. They seemed ter-ribly important. They were about saving women from being hurt or assaulted, about riding with a motorcycle gang as an outlaw (just like his brother did in real life), and about standing up to overzealous police and bullies. He didn't just tell stories, he became them, per-forming the various characters, mimicking their tones and gestures.

I listened in fascination. John was telling us who he was. He saw himself as a rebel, a loner, a tough guy, though I quickly learned that beneath his gruff exterior beat a sweet and vulnerable heart. John wanted to matter in this messed-up world. He lived on the edges, mis-understood and marginalized, but still he wanted to be a hero, to right wrongs, to save the day. But we never gave him that chance. We weren't really listening. We fed him, did his laundry, and played cribbage and crazy eights with him instead. And tried to teach him not to lie.

Fast-forward a couple of decades. Cancer had taken John, and his mother. A heroin overdose had taken his older brother years prior. And my part-time job had become a career. I was working for posAbilities, a large social service provider (by Canadian standards) that operates primarily in Metro Vancouver, British Columbia. I'd completed a master's degree in liberal studies, focusing on how language, power, and representation function in the disability space. For a philosophy nerd, this topic offered inflection points on an abundance of critical and far-reaching issues: society, personhood, citizenship, sexuality, genetics, history, rationality, autonomy, agency, morality, culture, power, deviancy, language, and so on. Yet it was, and continues to be, an area largely ignored by all the major disciplines, including the arts and humanities. That is a tragedy.

My curiosity about best and new practices led me to become an accreditation surveyor, working in a peer-based system that assessed how well organizations conformed to a set of evolving best practice

Too many people we worked with were living unwitnessed lives. They were ghosting through our communities, not part of community life. Not really.

standards. Not only did I apply the standards to organizations, I also occasionally helped draft new sections or standards for the manuals. This gave me lots of field exposure to social service agencies and programs throughout North America—a chance to see what others were trying and thinking. After a couple dozen surveys, however, I learned that our organizations were pretty much all the same, even though, perhaps unsurprisingly, each thought itself more or less unique.

We weren't unique. Nor were the lives of those we collectively supported. Too many people we worked with were living unwitnessed lives. They were ghosting through our communities, not part of community life. Not really. They showed up at parks, bowling halls, swimming pools, malls, and coffee shops, but there were rarely interactions with the public, even with staff in tow, maybe *because* staff were in tow. They had nowhere to go where people knew them, spoke to them, or missed them when they weren't there. Too many had no hobbies, jobs, or classes. And when they passed away, there would be some sort of remembrance ceremony, like John's, attended by a few staff and family—if they had family—but rarely any neighbours, co-workers, friends, family friends, old boyfriends or girlfriends, or others you might expect at a service.

Do I matter? This is, I think, perhaps the most rudimentary of existential questions. Answering it is the preoccupation of a lifetime.

The lives of the people we support certainly matter to their families, and to us. We know these people, care for them, and even love them. But is that enough for them to *matter*? Or is it an outrageous conceit to conflate mattering to us with a life that matters? What is a good life, a full life, if it isn't about participating in the grand project of being, immersing yourself in its glory and its struggle, and leaving footprints in the world and in the hearts of others? Real footprints, not imaginary ones. What could we do about that? What ought we do? These are the question that weighed on us, not only at posAbilities, but also at Kinsight and the Burnaby Association for Community Inclusion, two other social service providers in Metro Vancouver.

Although our organizations competed with one another for government contracts, and for the staff to deliver them, and although our histories together held some unpleasant politics, we came to trust one another and decided to co-invest in better outcomes for adults with intellectual disabilities and their families. Our partnership, which could be the subject of its own book, would be loosely formalized in 2017 as Degrees of Change.

It's important to note that we didn't come together because we were providing poor services. On the contrary, our organizations enjoyed good reputations with funders and families, and we routinely flew through accreditation, usually with exemplary mentions. We had an amazing complement of competent, caring, and dedicated staff, of whom we were immensely proud. We played various leadership roles in shaping and maturing the sector.

But after twenty-five years of our personal involvement, the adults in our programs were still living largely segregated and unfulfilling lives. They may not have known better, or been able to verbalize it, but we did and we could. They were rarely encircled by anyone save those paid to be there. They weren't well understood or celebrated by the public. They weren't part of the cornucopia of culture. And because we were attending more to their needs than to their potential, their futures became a derivative of the activities we set up for them. Of course, every organization has success stories that they can trot out. We did too. But these stories were not the norm, and the bar for what counted as a good story was too low.

We wanted so much more for the people in our programs, which would require so much more of ourselves. But how to begin? By combining our efforts as Degrees of Change, we wondered, could we get further?

After a couple decades of optimism, we had become disenchanted with our sector's rhetoric and our recycled conversations around inclusion, around the same sorts of "promising" pilots and workshops. The endless committees. The *au courant* jargon and training. The quality improvement loops and strategic planning cycles. The promissory note that said best practice standards would deliver better outcomes. The additions to the catalogue of services. These things weren't getting us where we wanted to go.

After a couple decades of optimism, we had become disenchanted with our sector's rhetoric and our recycled conversations around inclusion, around the same sorts of "promising" pilots and workshops.

What were we missing? How did we need to start thinking differently? We were eager to imagine and create the next generation of services, but we didn't know where to start. We resolved, really resolved, to try to figure that out.

A few years earlier I'd already withdrawn from my professional networks and connected instead with social innovation and social finance communities. I had stopped going to disability conferences and started showing up at gatherings on community development and social entrepreneurialism. I quit reading government or sectoral reports and instead devoured the works of community organizers, innovators, social economists, and philosophers. I gave up my office so that I could be in the community, where I suspected the answers lay, and where I could have different conversations with different people, in a setting other than an office or boardroom. And I sought out thought leaders from around the world to see which fresh ideas might help us unstick ourselves.

But some things are hard to unstick. The strident pursuit of efficiency cripples capacity. Risk aversion suffocates creativity and possibility, and it attenuates the power of the informal. There is a disastrous reluctance to invite community to be part of a solution when it is not "trained," when it doesn't have the "right" language or value set, when it cannot be reliably controlled or managed, and when it is characterized by uncertainty and unpredictability. In our need for control we tend to appropriate community as "volunteers," requiring background checks, creating unpaid positions or paid contracts, conducting risk assessments, and supplying training and supervision. In so doing, we colonize the informal, which spoils everything. We just end up replicating ourselves.

Our sector has an incredibly difficult time lifting people over our service fence so that they can live well in community. And sadly, there is virtually no one on the community side reaching out to pull them over.

That's why I recall being gobsmacked in 2013 when I first met Sarah Schulman and she told me about Family by Family, a model she'd co-created in Australia wherein families coach other families that are at risk of having their children removed from the home. The program has reduced removals by as much as eighty percent. If Sarah and the others behind her organization, InWithForward, could engage community to help solve problems involving children at risk, surely they could help us figure out how to tackle loneliness, disconnection, and the risks of inviting community to be part of the solution.

Once Degrees of Change partnered with InWithForward, we discovered that they didn't just truck in new methods. They were deep thinkers who helped us reframe our challenges. They posed provocative questions and intriguing alternatives. From them our organizations learned about cultural anthropology—paying attention to people's lived realities across contexts. We learned about human-centred design and how to source and apply social science theories to front-line practice. We thought we were finally on the way to something different.

All of the Degrees of Change executive directors committed time, resources, and permissions to the experiments we conducted ourselves and, later, with InWithForward (as you will see in Part II). We were thirsty for something better, and we knew we wouldn't get it using the same thinking and tool sets. But the effort to quench this particular thirst was utterly exhausting. It pushed all of us to our thresholds at least once, and it's probably taken years off our career lives. Social research and development, and innovation, is not all about creativity and having fun in the sandbox. It's arduous work. Serious work. It can bring relationships close to ruin. It's about feeling alone and misunderstood, about constantly wading against currents, about regularly managing conflict and aggrieved feelings. It's about precariousness and vulnerability and constantly stressing over finances. It's about peddling grand visions and opportunities to decision makers who don't see them or don't want them. It's about fear of exposure, fault-finding, and embarrassment. It's about weekly tensions between pragmatism and vision, caution and boldness, outputs and emergence. And it's about regularly falling short of ambitions.

Perhaps that's true of all passionate endeavours.

Yet we're still here, and we're hoping to lay down some track for our organizations to follow before we retire to cottage life, whatever that means to each of us. We called our three social service organizations Degrees of Change to reflect our hunch that system change will come from the accumulation of small changes, from new interactions, practices, and routines, not from fundamental policy shifts or large-scale solutions. Our sector is too saturated with long-held norms and values. It is too vast and interconnected, and too entrenched, and it lacks the competencies, resources, and cultures required to reimagine or reconstitute itself. It is too big to budge, but not too dense to permeate.

For us, and for me, true change is about a gradual but intentional shift in culture. That is a much longer-term proposition than the short-term disruptions often idealized by social innovators and philanthropic funders. Although it's harder to see or count, I believe that providing new kinds of interactions is the genesis to reinvigorating our collective imagination, our norms, and our expectations.

Sarah's story

LIKE GORD, I have a history of breaking the rules in order to remake them.

In 1996, a few years after Gord stumbled upon his career in the disability sector, I also found my calling: as a sting agent for the Texas Department of Health. I was twelve years old. What I lacked in height, I made up for in guts. I'd saunter into a bar or convenience store, place my purse on the counter, ask for a pack of Virginia Slims, and more often than not walk out with cigarettes in hand. The tobacco industry was the big bad guy. Statistics from my undercover buys were part of a nationwide effort to sue the industry for $206 billion and launch the biggest public health campaign ever.

By age fourteen, I was on to my second social startup, Game Over, convening groups of young people to create their own public health campaigns and write their own classroom curriculum on the dangers of smoking. That's when I had my first reckoning.

Tina was a year older and lived in the social housing complex down the street from our high school, an institution whose claim to

This big idea—starting with the users of programs, policies, or products—turned out to be the crux of human-centred design.

fame was its high teenage pregnancy rate, celebrated mariachi band, and Confederate mascot. Tina shared a ground floor apartment with her grandma, younger siblings, and a handful of cousins; her mom was in and out of the picture. To pay the bills, Tina's grandma left the house when it was still dark in the morning, and came back after it was dark in the evening. That left Tina to look after her brother, sister, and cousins—their school pick-ups and drop-offs, dinner, homework. Smoking was the least of her concerns. Sure, she knew cigarettes caused cancer, but they were her respite: smoke breaks afforded a few liberating minutes devoid of responsibilities. Tina wanted to know why I was the one deciding what was good and bad for her life. Spouting back a cost-benefit analysis of teenage smoking seemed rather moot. The point was: whose problem was I solving?

That question festered throughout university and graduate school as I veered away from the hard sciences and into the social sciences, curious about what shapes people's motivation, agency, and control. I wondered how we might develop programs and policies that started where people were at, rather than where experts wanted them to be. This big idea—starting with the users of programs, policies, or products—turned out to be the crux of human-centred design, a discipline I knew only in terms of making pretty objects: posters and toasters, logos and Lego, furniture and frocks.

It turns out that making an object such as a chair requires attentiveness to two things I'd missed in my earlier work: understanding both the users of the object, and the context for the object. To make a good chair, the designer must know who is sitting in the chair: their weight and height, whether they're a squirmy kid, a tired mother, or an older person with back pain. They must also know where the chair will be used. A formal dining room chair is different from a rec room recliner, which is different from an ergonomic desk chair. Both the user and the use case of the chair affect its specs and materiality. But designers don't stop at the concept. They move from a sketch of a chair to its three-dimensional form using a process called prototyping. They make a small-scale model of the chair to see if it works. Does it hold people's weight? Can it actually be made with available resources?

Tweaking the design of the chair before production and scale saves resources and reduces the risk of a crappy, unsafe item on the market.

What if we made social policy the way we make chairs? What if we understood the users of each policy and the context in which the policy would be implemented? What if we tested small-scale versions first?

These weren't just rhetorical questions. In 2007 I paused my doctoral program at Oxford University and teamed up with Participle, a first-of-its-kind design agency in London, England, to prototype new kinds of after-school supports for at-risk young people. We called our co-designed model Loops. Rather than spend time after school in age-segregated spaces like youth centres, young people could head to McDonald's or the barbershop and get connected to projects, work experience, and activities across the city. The prototype was successful, but the political climate wasn't hospitable to models that upended conventions around risk, health, safety, and labour management.

Over the next five years, together with designers Chris Vanstone, Jonas Piet, and Muryani, I set up design teams in Australia and the Netherlands to make and test alternative supports for families in the child protection system, older caregivers, and women escaping domestic violence. Some of these alternatives still exist. Family by Family in Australia, for example, links families who've been through tough times with families currently in the throes of a tough time. Yet scaled success stories have been rare. Project after project, we kept hitting the same stumbling blocks. We were headstrong, impatient, and at times willfully naive. Not surprisingly, we antagonized the incumbents, raising the ire of social service organizations that had large government contracts and trusting funder relationships. We struggled to find organizations willing and able to finance or implement the new models coming out of our design processes. Without owners for our fledgling ideas, or the political capital to free up financial and human resources, our promising concepts too often floundered.

A moment of deliberate serendipity changed that. In 2013 Al Etmanski, the renowned disability advocate, community organizer, and social innovator, hosted a series of social innovation workshops in

Victoria and Vancouver. He invited InWithForward, the organization
I co-founded in the Netherlands and which I currently lead, to share
some of our failures and ambitions.

It was my first introduction to the Canadian landscape—and to the
social service organizations behind Degrees of Change. At one of the
events I literally ran into Gord, spilling wine and sparking conversation. Within nine months of that first encounter, our InWithForward
team was packing our bags and flying from Rotterdam to Vancouver. We knew this wasn't a perfunctory business arrangement when
Gord and Christine Scott, executive director of Kinsight, picked us
up at the airport in a minivan and drove us to our new home: apartment 303 in a social housing complex in Burnaby, British Columbia.
It was the start of many profoundly warm and personal interactions
to come. Over the next three months we shared macaroni and cheese,
dumplings, kabobs, and pizza with most of our neighbours, including
residents with developmental disabilities, getting to know their tastes
and the makeup of their days, nights, and weekends.

Why? Because we had been invited.

The Degrees of Change partners were not content with the way
things were. They were not content with the loneliness, the isolation,
the downgraded expectations, and the narrow aspirations of so many
adults with disabilities. And that was extraordinary. Never before
had we met leaders with the same mix of vulnerability and courage.
Indeed, we had never started with an admission that not only is the
status quo unsatisfactory, it is too often sustained by the organizational structures set up to do good. Yes, broader systems are at play.
The flow of dollars and accountabilities can freeze thinking and practice in place. But the status quo is not only a resourcing problem; the
status quo is also an imagination problem.

The very idea of social welfare needs reimagining.

We, Degrees of Change and InWithForward, shared this sentiment and saw it not as an academic platitude but as a joint call to
action. Making better versions of the existing practice just wasn't cut-
ting through the existential malaise. Across the different geographies
where InWithForward worked, one thing was sadly ordinary: the

colourless lives that the welfare state set people up to lead. Whether it was British youth who'd never seen the sea despite growing up in housing projects a short drive away, or South Australian families lost within the child protection system, or Dutch women uncertain how to rebuild their lives in a domestic violence shelter, or Canadian adults with developmental disabilities passing their time in malls and vans, the welfare state operated with remarkable consistency. It assessed vulnerabilities, diagnosed deficiencies, doled out labels, amassed expertise, filed plans, and set limits.

Jen, whom I first met outside of Adelaide, South Australia, dreamed of a limitless world. But first she had to prove her fitness as a mother. When I met her, she was sitting on the floor with her rambunctious two-year-old son, pushing a toy train. Her social worker was filming them. "See how you checked out there and broke your eye contact?" the social worker asked, replaying the video. Jen nodded and looked down, seemingly embarrassed. The social worker changed tack and offered praise for the remnants of the healthy breakfast on the kitchen table.

There appeared to be no limits to the social worker's gaze. But as Jen soon found out, there were limits to her own gaze. When I asked where she saw herself in a year, she spoke of travelling abroad with her son. Ireland was on her bucket list. Back at the office, however, the social worker gave Jen a high-risk score. Jen's travel comment had struck the worker as "hopelessly naive," indicating a lack of forethought and parental responsibility. "She's not taking being a mother seriously," the social worker commented, concerned that this was part of a behavioural pattern that could put Jen's son on the path to removal.

InWithForward plays a different role than that of social workers or other direct service providers. Our role isn't to intervene in the present. Our role is to co-design interventions for the future. When we ask people like Jen to describe the supports they want, they can often speak to the function but not the form. Jen wants to travel and have more agency over her choices, but she doesn't have ready examples for what that looks like or how to get there. What people know to ask

Across the different geographies where InWithForward worked, one thing was sadly ordinary: the colourless lives that the welfare state set people up to lead.

for is shaped by what they have seen and heard and what they can fathom. The narrower their contexts, the fewer reference points they may have and the more constricted their field of possibility.

As social designers, we can come up with fresh ideas and visualize alternative support models in the same way that a designer might sketch and mock up a chair. But in doing so, we often give voice to preferences and aspirations that run counter to the stated goals of the service system. For example, when we draw a storyboard for a travel service that connects Jen to families around the world, we rub against the system's definition of risk and responsibility.

Our social service system counts only certain needs—for safety, shelter, food, income, and physical care. It has few ways of understanding people's needs for adventure, purpose, connection, or growth. Intake forms generally don't include boxes people can tick to express their capabilities, skills, or hopes. Without this fuller picture, it's all too easy for service providers and their clients to fall into the binary of helper and helpee, and all too hard for people like Jen to retain a sense of competence and control over their story.

The three-month project that InWithForward began in 2014, to paint a fuller picture of the residents of that Burnaby housing complex, turned into a five-year experiment with Gord and the Degrees of Change agencies to redefine the very intents and purposes of social welfare. It was during those five years of trial, error, and more trial that the plot lines of this book emerged.

Flourishing lives

This book shares the questions, hunches, practical projects, and learning that have come from the multi-year partnership between three established non-profits (Degrees of Change) and one social design organization (InWithForward).

We are strange bedfellows. Most of our journey together has been unplanned and off-road. What you'll read in this book is more than a summary of our travels. You'll read about the movements—what we

call stretches—that we believe are necessary if the social service system is to serve as a staging area for human development and collective
potential, loosening itself from the triage trap in which it's currently
caught.

The goal we have been journeying toward is, simply, flourishing
lives—lives in which growth and actualization are taken as seriously
as safety and stability.

This proposition may be a non-starter for you, depending on your
role in the social services. If you're with government or a service
delivery organization, you may feel that supporting self-realization
isn't your job, that it's up to individuals to reach their potential, that a
flourishing life is a nice-to-have rather than a must-have. If resources
are frequently scarce in your environment, you might see spending
money on more than the "basics" as unrealistic—even irresponsible.

If you're a social justice advocate, you may find it hard to defend
the raised benchmark too. It's one thing to seek equal treatment under
the law and pursue equal access to benefits and services. It could be
another, or so you may think, to argue for a right to public spending
on "higher order" outcomes.

Whether we address the goal of flourishing lives within a rights,
duty, or economic framework, is it something we ought to do? This is
a consequential question: a lot hangs on the answer.

We would argue that focusing exclusively on immediate needs is
an ineffective and inefficient use of resources. It may even be unethical. Here are some of our reasons for saying so.

- Servicing people's immediate needs without attention to their
  deeper needs for agency and control can create dependencies
  and stall progress. The transactional nature of exchanges between
  those who help and those who are helped can trap people in their
  realities. We feel good when we feed the hungry and house the
  homeless, all too easily reaffirming rather than recalibrating the
  power imbalances that perpetuate inequality.

- Immediate and deeper needs are very much intertwined, despite
  misleading language that suggests one is more primary than

Our social service system counts only certain needs— for safety, shelter, food, income, and physical care. It has few ways of understanding people's needs for adventure, purpose, connection, or growth.

another. Although we tend to privilege immediate needs because they're more urgent, obvious, and treatable, they are rooted in soils that are personal, cultural, and historical. The story of hunger is not merely about someone trying to figure out how to survive; it's the story of world-making and who gets to be part of it and who doesn't. It's not merely the story of the body, it is also a story of the soul.

- Directing resources only to the neediest becomes a never-ending race to the bottom. Services end up using their resources to manage crisis after crisis, rather than leveraging resources for social and economic return.

- Asking staff of social service agencies to attend only to immediate needs can be dehumanizing. It segments people into categories of needs and entitlements, and it discourages staff from seeing or discharging their personal moral duties to the people they come into contact with.

We see social welfare as a collective social responsibility, not the exclusive domain of government or any particular service sector. But because the social sector already has relationships in community and with people on the margins, and because it's already funded and pointed toward social outcomes, we are well placed to cultivate interventions and networks that lead to good lives. The "we" includes anyone with a role in social services: government or service delivery organizations, social justice advocates or policy analysts, board members or foundation directors, family of people who receive services or staff who work directly with them. Immediate needs are important for all of us, but if that is the acme of our ambition, we have surrendered all hope of change or transformation.

Experiments, not answers

Work in human services is complicated and messy, no matter how much we try to make it clean and clear. Whether you are a philanthropist trying to weigh the best investments in social impact, a policy analyst trying to make sense of research and political mandates, a program evaluator trying to count what matters, a government official weighing needs against resource allocations, an organizational leader wrestling with strategy, a front-line worker trying to discern where your organizational duties end and your personal duties begin, or a family member struggling to understand your role in another's present and future—you're unlikely to say this is easy, straightforward stuff. What we talk about in this book isn't neat and tidy either, but we do think it's relevant to what you do.

Throughout these pages, you'll see us posing questions but rejecting simple answers. You'll find us acknowledging tensions that exist in our system but working *with* them rather than against them. This inquiry-led approach may sound abstract, but we hope to show you that it's deeply pragmatic. During our partnership, it has biased us toward action and has liberated us to try things and see what sticks. We've tried big things, like reinventing front-line roles, developing new back-end technologies, and flipping the volunteer experience on its head. We've tried small things, like rewriting job ads, changing intake forms, and introducing tools to spark fresh conversations.

Which interventions prompt deeper change, we've wondered, and for whom, and when? Our experiments have trended toward the disruptive—approaches that embody a different logic from that of the dominant system, and that are categorically or qualitatively different from present best practices. Because we've set flourishing lives as the outcome, we accept that the interventions we co-design may run counter to prevailing beliefs and assumptions.

Yet we have never pursued disruption as the end point. Our approaches don't have to be world-altering, we've realized. They need only be different enough from the usual anatomy of a service or policy that they produce a generative tension that pulls us toward new values, in a way that makes it impossible to go back to how things were. For every small shift, we no longer see things the same way anymore. We start talking differently and imagining differently. It's the accumulation of small shifts that we believe can lead to system change.

Immediate needs are important for all of us, but if that is the acme of our ambition, we have surrendered all hope of change or transformation.

The experiments we describe in this book, and the twelve stretches we propose for reimagining the social services, are not theoretical musings. They come from our on-the-ground experiences as non-profit service delivery agencies. As we've tried one thing and then another, we have tested the limits of our flexibility and adaptability. How much can we augment what we currently do with what we feel we *ought* to do? To what extent are renewed relationships—with the people who use our services, our employees, the surrounding community, government funders, accrediting bodies, philanthropists, organized labour—within our reach or beyond it?

We've discovered that we need to do more than come up with path-breaking interventions. We need to fashion an environment that is spry enough, that can stretch enough, to accommodate the constant contortions required to usher in a different future for our sector.

What's to come

This book is divided into three parts.

In Part I, we briefly trace the history of social services in Canada. We show how, in the pursuit of fairness, the system has prioritized sameness: using rules, training regimes, and quality assurance frameworks to erase the ambiguity that's inherent in working with humans. We explain how we've come to regard tension as a creative force that opens up the field of options and gives us room to imagine and test new models. We introduce our so-called stretch approach, which argues for preserving tensions rather than resolving or "curing" them. When we preserve tensions, we can ask more incisive questions and practice greater discernment.

In Part II, we share some of the experiments that Degrees of Change and InWithForward collaborated on as we tried to piece together new ways of doing what we do. Some of our experiments succeeded a little, some not at all. Yet we feel it's important to share the results of our work, positive or otherwise. In all cases we learned important lessons about the kind of environment it takes to enable lives to flourish.

In Part III, we describe the twelve stretches that we think, over time, will both reinvigorate our work and lead us to systems that are more human. We also pose "stretch questions" to help you reflect on how each stretch might be relevant to you and your role in the social services. The stretches fall into three categories:

1 **Stretching our focuses:** Social services typically assign resources to needs they consider basic, such as safety, shelter, food, clothing, life skills, and physical health. But this is only part of life. What about the part that involves meaning, beauty, and identity? We propose stretching the focuses of our work so that we attend to both parts.

2 **Stretching our roles:** Social services tend to be inward-facing, conceived and delivered by a coterie of professionals and predicated on the assumption that we are the ones to supply the solutions. We explore ways of stretching our roles so that we can augment our service-heavy model with one that allows informal solutions to take hold, that activates community capacity, and that helps people navigate a life out in the world.

3 **Stretching our frameworks:** If we reimagine our focuses and our roles, we also need to rethink the frameworks and systems that support them. These stretches may be especially challenging because they're about large system adaptations, about retooling and repurposing our infrastructure, workforce, services, and strategies.

At the end of the book is a plain language summary of our proposed stretches, because we recognize that our language may not be accessible to some. There is also a list of all the stretch questions so that you can consider them together.

The twelve stretches we propose represent the joint vision of the organizations in our multi-year partnership. But that is where full agreement ends. This book does not presume to speak for everyone in our partnership. While there are many overlaps between our views, as authors, and those of other partners and participants in this journey with us, there are also real differences.

Some of the stories, critiques, and analyses in this book may hurt, offend, or anger some readers. That's not our intention. We frequently struggle with how to talk about difficult topics without alienating anyone. On the one hand, we want to draw your attention to the limits of the current system. On the other, we don't want to dishonour the extraordinary people who work within it. Provocation can both expand understanding and repel people, and it's hard to find the right setting on the dial. In the end, we feel an acute and urgent responsibility to those on the margins of our society who are not doing well and who need many things to change. Today. If we push too hard, doors will close. If we don't push hard enough, doors won't open. That's why we feel compelled to share with you our stories and our hard-won insights.

Neither is it our intention to disparage organizations or systems, though we're probably guilty of that at times. We're not looking to antagonize the social service system. Yes, the obduracy of institutions can be frustrating and sometimes embittering. It's a complicated mash of helpful and unhelpful that we are trying to sift through, not only in the systems we're trying to affect, but also in our thinking and approaches. If you sometimes detect ambivalence in our writing, it's because it's there. But we are fundamentally hopeful.

Many of the examples and stories in this book are drawn from the intellectual disability sector because that's where many of our partners work; others are drawn from InWithForward's experiences working within homelessness, mental health, domestic violence, older age, and immigrant services. Organizations within the social sector share similar roles and structures; we all exist in a tenuous web of dogma and realpolitik. You must be the judge of what applies and what doesn't to your patch of the social service world.

In writing this book, we're not suggesting that we've figured everything out and that you should do as we have. Far from it. We are struggling, as individuals and as organizations. We're nowhere near as good at stretching as we would like to be. And we are tired. The work we do is strenuous, and meaningful change doesn't come easily. At no point do we mean to dismiss the values, thinking, programs, and innovations that have gotten us to where we are now. We know that we can envisage the future only while standing on the shoulders of those who brought us to the present—families who fought for their loved ones, and deep thinkers and humanitarians who made it their life's work to leave something better behind. For them, and for all they have done, we are humbled and grateful. Lastly, we acknowledge that our work has taken place on the unceded lands of Indigenous peoples. If only this fledgling nation had spent more time learning about their relationships to the land, people, and the sacred, and less time trying to strip that away from them.

I

Beginnings, Undertakings, and Take-Aways

Always question the "why"; don't be satisfied with only knowing the "how."

CATHERINE PULSIFER

SEMA TREATED DOLMA-MAKING as a serious craft. She stuffed grape leaves with a mixture of minced lamb and mint, and doused them in a thick tomato sauce seasoned with cumin. But her handiwork was increasingly interrupted by phone calls and door knocks. On the other end might be her housing worker, her employment worker, her children's social worker, or her domestic violence worker. Sema worried that not answering could be a strike against her, evidence that could be used to remove her kids or downgrade her welfare benefits.

A year earlier, Sema felt on the cusp of regaining her freedom. She had masterminded a daring escape out of Turkey, where she and her kids were forced into domestic slavery by her husband and his parents. And yet the domestic violence shelter in the Netherlands where Sema ended up also felt like a prison. There, her interactions were monitored and her temporary suite was overlooked by the workers' corporate offices.

Moving into her own apartment didn't make much difference. Sema couldn't control when professionals called. She couldn't control how they assessed her state of mind, her parenting style, or her choice of activities. With her days eaten up by mandated appointments, Sema had little time to reconnect with family, forge new friendships, or even take her kids to the playground.

Sema's front-line workers and their managers also felt they had little control. They were trying hard to do good, and they often did. But was it good enough? They suffered from burnout and compassion fatigue, painful byproducts of a desire to help in an environment where needs always seemed to outstrip available resources.

1

Loosening the flotilla

ERIC TRIST, CO-FOUNDER of the Tavistock Institute of Human Relations, once characterized complex systems as a flotilla of ships, connected beneath the waterline by a flexible iron cord. The social service ecosystem is like that. It consists of massive ships, almost flotillas of their own, such as government and labour; mid-sized ships such as service delivery organizations, educational institutions, professional associations, and accreditation bodies; and small ships of families, users, and community members.

What happens to this flotilla when there is urgency to set a new direction? Nothing quick. Or, more likely, nothing at all. A powerful inertia exists because of the sheer mass of all those vessels, many of them large and unwieldy, travelling in the same direction for so long. Systems and methodologies become so firmly entrenched that they're no longer visible or contestable. They are just the way things are done.

An individual like Sema, whom you met at the opening of these chapters, doesn't have enough pull to reorient an organization, never mind a flotilla. Nor do the employees. All are swept along the same course.

How, then, do we push through the stagnation? Especially if we don't think the urgency of the problem is shared by all the ships in the flotilla? Especially if those ships have different imperatives, needs, and perspectives? How do we take a situation like Sema's and make of it a joint departure point?

Systems are still a vital organizing framework so long as they remain connected to, and are drawing nourishment from, moral roots of equity and equality.

In the work we've done, both inside and outside the disability sector, we've seen how so many of our systems and structures are more or less adrift in the present, without capacity to learn from the past or reimagine the future. They're focused on two things: identifying and responding to crisis, and consistently delivering what they say they will. We've seen how our cultures can strangle versatility and dexterity and lock us into endless patterns of system consolidation. Strategic planning, continuous quality improvement, pilot programs—these are all variations of the same thing. They draw from the same well of data (satisfaction surveys, focus groups, demographic trends, and so forth). They enlist input from the same people using the usual questions and import the same historical values and assumptions.

The goal? To make organizations and systems a little more efficient, a little more effective, a little more satisfying. How? Through more checks and balances, policies, procedures, roles, programs, data collection, and training. More of the same.

How do we get unstuck? How do we get better at identifying the gaps between what is said and what is done, between what is needed and what is supplied, and between what is deemed worthwhile and what is measured? And how do we communicate those gaps so that they translate across all components of the system and sound a joint call to action?

We believe that if all of us in the social services can collectively stretch in similar ways, we'll loosen the iron cord that ties us all together, without severing it. Systems are still a vital organizing framework so long as they remain connected to, and are drawing nourishment from, moral roots of equity and equality. By stretching the connections that bind us, by working with the tensions in our systems and ourselves, we think we can move in a new direction, one that acknowledges history while freeing us up to chart a different sort of future.

―――

THE WORK OF a paid carer, whether it's a domestic violence worker, housing worker, aged care worker or disability support worker, originated largely from the work of women in the home. Caring for the vulnerable was initially viewed as a natural act, coming from a place of compassion, rather than a professional function tied to deep skill or expertise.

That started to shift in the 1960s with the postwar rise of caring occupations such as social work, and social workers' growing push for professional status and higher pay. To be a professional was to *not* be an amateur: it meant to do a job well, to use sound judgement, to demonstrate ethical behaviour. Yet despite the formation of standard curricula and peer associations, social work and the other caring occupations never rose to the status of medicine or law. The training was shorter. The specialized know-how was seen as smaller. You can have privileged communication with a doctor or lawyer, but not with a social worker or front-line worker. Indeed, what traditionally characterized the high-status professions was their level of discretion, autonomy, and authority. They were entrusted to do the right thing at the right time. That was not the case for professional caregivers, who were expected to follow care protocols set and monitored by others.

By the 1970s and 1980s, a new ideology took hold. Managerialism brought a different value set to professionalism and altruism—namely, optimization, efficiency, and pragmatism. Managers knew best. By restructuring, aligning incentives, and increasing the number and role of managers, organizations could maximize their resources. The organization, rather than the individual or the professional, became a crucial unit of focus.

2

The rise of
the professional

THIS HISTORY EXPLAINS how the social services have ended up where they are: born out of compassion, striving for professional legitimacy, and tasked with resource allocation and rationalization. And it begins to explain how people like Sema come to be treated within the service web.

As valuable as professionalism and managerialism have been for our field, they risk dehumanizing what we do. This is because creating coordinated systems requires the suppression of the individual in favour of consistency and efficiency. Over time, organizational apparatuses grow so large that they squeeze out the personal. This trend, while understandable, is particularly unsettling when our purpose is *people*. The front-line worker becomes an increasing perplexity: an employee with motives and feelings that are very much human, and a fair bit more complicated than just empathy or concern; a professional with limited stature or authority; and a labour resource that chafes against being treated as a mere resource.

Professional codes of conduct are supposed to help the front-line worker manage this perplexity. Codes of conduct, adapted from private sector practice and soon copied by the public sector, were intended to translate values into more visible behaviours. However, their impact has been mixed. On the one hand, employees will apparently do what they do, regardless of what's contained in the codes. On the other hand, codes are part of training curricula, and practitioners may turn to them for guidance in navigating complex terrain.

Front-line work is often turbulent and chaotic. Without clear standards and boundaries, people can get hurt and even traumatized. Codes of ethics establish boundaries, in part to reduce emotional and relational entanglements. But there's a double edge to the codes and the ethical clarity they seek to accomplish. While our moral questions ultimately revolve around people's relatedness, our professional codes answer those questions with separation. Codes draw fortified circles around us so that we cannot spill out and others cannot spill in. They create distance when what's needed is authentic connection, and they convert moral interactions into transactional ones.

Interventions, especially in the social sector, are mediated by relationships. Our work is not just about programs and techniques, but about how these things are delivered and experienced. Sometimes the intervention is not the intervention, but is instead an exquisite moment of human encounter that brings with it hope, beauty, and inspiration. Sometimes the answer is not a rule or a professional demeanour, but is instead love and vulnerability.

Workers are more than technicians, and the people who use our services are more than the needs they present. We are all made of water, not stone. Our being is rooted in relationships, not professional discourses. The philosopher Gabriel Marcel goes so far as to say that the self is constituted by relationships, that we cannot be understood outside the relationships that went into our making—our family, friends, children, mentors, adversaries, and so on. To *be* is being-with-others; this is an axiom of our existence. That's why we must find the right blend of technique and love, of being professional and being personal. Otherwise, we run the risk of dehumanizing everyone in the interaction.

We believe it is vital to inject soul into bureaucracy—and to do it boldly and without apology—before power, accountability, and efficiency completely annex the glory of being-with-others.

We believe it is vital
to inject soul into
bureaucracy—and to do
it boldly and without
apology—before power,
accountability, and
efficiency completely
annex the glory of
being-with-others.

3

How the flotilla got stuck

THE SOCIAL WELFARE state emerged in Canada in the mid-twentieth century in order to bring stability, security, and prosperity to a country still reeling from a world war, the Great Depression, and the deflation of the national currency. High poverty and unemployment rates led to a series of federal and provincial interventions such as unemployment insurance and housing assistance.

These early social reforms signalled an emerging role for government in the social sector. Over time, government programs burgeoned to include disability supports, child welfare, employment assistance, and an expanded role in health and education. Social welfare—the idea that we look after our most vulnerable—became a defining Canadian value, so much so that we enshrined it in our legislation and government institutions. Social welfare was no longer left to the discretionary purview of caring individuals, charities, and private organizations. Philanthropic organizations still bestow considerable social and financial benefit to communities, either by delivering government mandates or by addressing gaps, but they are no longer the principal ships in the flotilla.

As Canada's social welfare system developed, a notable split occurred. Policy and funding, set and provided by government, became separated from delivery, contracted out to an ever-growing

What we have today
is a cracked and over-
burdened old-world
system that has not
evolved to address new-
world circumstances.

number of social service agencies. With that separation, systemic change became a lot more confounding and daunting.

There are now in the order of 20,000 social service providers across Canada, delivering everything from outreach supports for people living on the streets to community inclusion programs for adults with intellectual disabilities. Which organization, or which collection of organizations, can steer us in a new direction? Where can a change platform come from, and how can it translate across thousands of independent organizations, jurisdictions, and service sectors?

It's tempting to think that government might provide such a platform, but it's hard for us to see how. Funding for social services is splintered across so many federal, provincial, and municipal bodies, each ensconced in their own political cycles, cultures, and pressures, that it's nearly impossible for governments to act in a cohesive way. While US Supreme Court Associate Justice Louis Brandeis saw divided government as an opportunity to produce "laboratories of democracy," there does not appear to be any ready mechanism in social service work that can harness the generative capacity of fragmentation.

TODAY, FIFTY OR sixty years after social welfare reform began in Canada, the world is an incredibly different place. Science and technology have irrevocably changed human civilization, solving some problems but introducing hosts of new ones. Data production and availability—and abuse—are growing exponentially. Urbanization is giving rise to all sorts of health, environmental, social, cultural, and economic effects. Climate warming is desolating places and economies throughout the world. Social conflicts are displacing, starving, and murdering millions of people. Global capitalism continues to widen the gap between the rich and the poor.

Simply put, the social sector hasn't kept pace. It has expanded its volume and scope and bulked up its accountability, but not its generative ability. You could do a taste test of programs across agencies, geographies, and time and not find a whole lot of variation. There have been incremental tweaks, but little that's been disruptive—nothing that remotely matches the stupefying pace of innovation in technology and commerce.

This lag might be fine if social services were responding well to social challenges and delivering great outcomes, but that would be a difficult position to defend. Instead of ongoing adaptation and innovation, we're seeing our infrastructure thicken and ossify to the point where people like Sema spend too much time satisfying the needs of the system and too little time satisfying their needs as humans. We're seeing our services, which should be able to accommodate people where they're at, stiffen into generic moulds.

In our experience, this sectoral stuckness throughout social services is intensified by other problems, like too much self-importance and too little self-interrogation. Too much jockeying, positioning, and organizational protectionism. Too many comparisons with other organizations and sectoral standards, and not enough comparisons against bold visions. There are enough structural impediments hindering our work: strain on limited resources and capacities, overwork and fatigue, too much expected of too little. We must be careful to not compound a paucity of resources with a paucity of humility, curiosity, or ambition.

What we have today is a cracked and overburdened old-world system that has not evolved to address new-world circumstances. The cracks have been there for a while, even if they haven't been in the light.

4

Institutions, old and new

OR NEARLY A hundred years, the best practice for "atypical" children and adults was to house them in institutions and asylums. At the time, concentrating expertise in one place for a segment of the population that was not well understood was considered enlightened thinking. On the advice of doctors, families sent brothers, sisters, and children with developmental disabilities and mental illnesses to institutions in the hope that they'd receive specialized care and treatment. Many grew up, grew old, and died in these institutions, often without grave markers to bear witness to their final resting place. Eventually, though, families like these started to ask tough questions and challenge basic assumptions, principal among them this: why is life in these institutions better than life with us?

In British Columbia institutions began closing in earnest in the 1970s and 1980s. As people with intellectual disabilities moved back into the community, optimism swelled. Children and adults with intellectual disabilities would have a chance to live a normal life, not one manufactured in an institution. They could step out from the confines of fluorescent lights and cinder block walls and become valued members of their communities and citizens of society.

Out of the institutional ruins, families constructed alternatives. They banded together to set up associations, buy homes, and decentralize supports. Instead of psychiatrists and nurses, they hired people who had little to no experience but the right value sets. The language of deformity and deficiency was gradually discarded in favour of the language of dignity, strengths, and rights.

As the community living movement grew, value-driven practice evolved into rule-driven practice. By the 1990s informality had given way to formality. Post-secondary certificates, diplomas, and degrees for training in the disability sector had emerged. Professional designations and expectations were increasing. Job classifications and funding formulas were becoming more standardized. In the 2000s, accreditation, which assessed organizations against best practice standards, became a requirement for organizations in British Columbia with government contracts exceeding $500,000. Today there are close to 1,200 standards that apply to our organizations. Policy, procedural, and governance manuals thickened. Handbooks and service catalogues were created for consumers, along with bills of rights and codes of ethics. Written plans and reports covered every imaginable scenario: care, accessibility, quality improvement, barrier reduction, strategy, operations, technology, and more. It was all about providing better services, safer services, more efficient services. The sector was "maturing."

In our naïveté we discovered too late that an institution is more than those cinder blocks and fluorescent lights. It's a way of thinking about and organizing the world. Before long, we were bemoaning the fact that we had closed large institutions only to open many smaller ones. How could that happen?

AN ORGANIZATION IS misguided if it thinks it manages its own culture. Just as a tree perched on a coastal bluff is bent by its environment, so too are our organizations. Statutory and contractual obligations determine what goes into the policy manual, what sorts of roles and functions exist, and what training follows. Complicated work requires complicated processes that everyone needs to adhere to. Not so

Too few are asking whether the current system ought to be sustained as it is. Is it working?

suddenly, and not so surprisingly, safety, consistency, and compliance become primary cultural features. And that's just the beginning. Busyness, scant resources, and the constant need for problem solving take time away from the deeper, longer work of reflecting on purposes, values, and vision.

As long as we're bound by organizational and professional requirements, we remain stuck in the orbit of system operations, immersed in their languages, logics, and imperatives. These forces shape the cultural bedrock of almost any organization.

Looking at the extensive systems now in place for both adults and children, we could argue that children's services have fared better. There, the accent has fallen on childhood development and growth. There's an appreciation not only of safety but also of learning and actualization. The assumption is that children have real potential, which can be unlocked by the constellation of professionals who have appeared for that purpose: speech therapists, early childhood educators, behaviour therapists, infant and child development consultants, and family support workers, to name a few. Sadly, when these children grow up and enter the world of adult services, the accent shifts from personal growth back to safety. The assumption seems to be that it's too late for adults to realize their potential.

What fuels this assumption? When did we, as social service providers, decide to leave family homes, schools, and neighbourhoods and instead work out of program sites? How is it that we stopped applying a developmental mindset once people turned eighteen or nineteen years old? When did routine and redirection become ubiquitous features of services?

Cost is one reason. The social sector has seen its share of budgetary expansions and contractions, but pressures are rising. Higher health care costs coupled with more boomers retiring changes the financial picture. At the same time, there is greater demand for social services. When there are insufficient public funds to meet demand, pressure is continuously applied on organizations to stretch budgets as far as possible. The general public is often unaware of just how much the social sector does, or tries to do, and how little they have to do it with. Nevertheless, a series of revisions to funding formulas in the past decade has left many community living service providers gasping. Irrespective of the rationale, these funding adjustments can have the effect of straining critical infrastructure. And that often means that growth, learning, and the movement toward self-realization must take a back seat to stabilizing crises and maintaining minimum levels of service for the most people possible, no matter how vapid and generic those services may be.

In each cycle of contraction, the vexing problem of system sustainability enters virtually all of our conversations. Mostly we commiserate about how difficult things have become, how the government is forfeiting its obligations, and what political, media, fundraising, or social finance strategies might get us out of this fix. Too few are asking whether the current system ought to be sustained as it is. Is it working? Is it performing well enough that all it needs is more money to extend its impact?

We don't think so. It's not that simple.

5

Living and dying systems

ERE IS THE not-so-secret thing: all systems eventually become obsolete. They lose relevance as the conditions that gave rise to them shift, as demographic trends reshape fiscal realities, as new technologies emerge, and as moral sensibilities evolve. Just look at the death of land lines, video stores, and, in many jurisdictions, taxis.

The death of institutions gave birth to many new social service organizations and to the community living sector. Now the novelty of group homes and day programs is wearing off. Where once those innovations signalled a paradigm shift from institutional to community life, today we find ourselves noticing the gaps between what was hoped for and what was achieved. After half a century of deinstitutionalization, the community model has accumulated its own dogmas, conventions, and structures, which are causing it to become stuck. It's tempting to construe the growing demand for services, along with the widespread use of consumer satisfaction surveys, as validation of those services. And in the absence of any real alternatives, or any serious investigation of outcomes, that conjecture can't be challenged, which only results in further consolidation of the system.

As with institutional care, we can expect current care models to *eventually* fall into disrepair, even after holding on much longer than they would have in the private market.

The first question is: how do we know when a model or system is beginning to surpass its usefulness? How do we sift through all the signals to know something is failing and, rather than rallying to prop it up, learn to let it go? In our experience, quality improvement exercises and strategic planning, even when dressed up in the language of innovation and change management, run the risk of prolonging the life of moribund systems. They don't peel back the logics and values that keep things as they are, and they don't invest in the sort of data that can make basic assumptions visible and contestable. When there is analysis, the distinction between what's worth keeping and what needs to be discarded is too often superficial and perfunctory.

The second question is: what will replace the institutional models of today—the residential group homes, homeless shelters, soup kitchens, drop-in centres, nursing homes, and halfway houses? What will be salvaged and what will be changed? Who will be involved with families? What will the roles of the future look like? And who will decide?

As we discuss in Part II, tackling such questions has made us look both outside the sector, at the ways in which communities and industries in distress have reformulated themselves, and inside the sector, re-examining who is at the centre of our work and why we do what we do. Our hope is that by stretching our sensibilities, we can thoughtfully create a *next* logic for the social services, one that resists homogeneity and convention and instead installs space for experimentation and creativity.

6

Stretching or innovating?

ERE, WE INTRODUCE stretching as a way to loosen up the social welfare flotilla. In Part II we get practical and describe the on-the-ground projects that have taught us how to be more limber. In Part III we propose twelve stretches that, we believe, can reshape the social sector.

Throughout, we use the term "stretching" deliberately. It is not, for us, a synonym for innovating. Innovation has a built-in positive bias. It assumes new things are good things—that is, until the consequences of the new things become hard to ignore. Look at Facebook, Airbnb, and Uber. They were introduced with fanfare and held up as the very definition of social progress, in large part by outpacing existing regulatory frameworks. All three are now beset with profound ethical quandaries. They have thoroughly expanded corporate power and have reshaped—without democratic debate—privacy, elections, urban planning, and labour protections. Still, all three have growing customer bases, with loyal followers who can't fathom daily life without the connections and convenience their products provide.

That's the thing: innovations are neither wholly good nor wholly bad. It depends on how they're used, the outcomes they enable for whom, and how the winners and losers stack up. It depends on motivation and context.

Stretching recognizes that motivation and context. It starts with where you're at, inflexibilities and all, and slowly moves you toward another position. Stretching is therefore an ongoing act, not merely a characteristic. Implied in the notion of a stretch is the sense of extending yourself from one state toward a different state. Stretching isn't easy. Baked into the word is an appreciation that it takes energy and can feel uncomfortable, asking us to confront supposed limits and constraints. This has certainly been our experience when questioning entrenched logics and leaning toward alternatives.

The corollary to social innovation's positive bias to new things is its casual disregard of old things. The push for novelty can leave little room for understanding or appreciating history. Stretching does not ignore the past. We can stretch backward and forward. That's why we have to understand the movements that led our sector to this point before we can try out some new twists. If we are to build more flexibility, more flow, more capacity into our otherwise staid and intransigent structures, we need to respect where those structures came from and recognize the important role they presently play, along with the people who currently indwell them.

There's a romantic notion that social progress is a kind of punctuated evolution in which discrete, disruptive innovations come along, topple the past, and install something new, or in which products are developed in research labs, plugged into the field, and scaled. This notion largely ignores the role of continuous adaptation, growth, and relationships in human history.

In our experience, social innovation evangelists tend to be a little too enamoured with products and services that can be scaled out—or with far-reaching policies that can be scaled up—in order to deliver uniform effects like cultural transformation and system change. Innovation and growth have come to be synonymous. The assumption is that new things, once validated by local demand, should expand. Smaller adaptations, tweaks to interactions, and localized solutions are too often seen as nice but not systemic.

But you can tip a boat with a boulder or with gravel. And gravel is more manageable. By being engrossed in only grand things, we

By being engrossed in only grand things, we underappreciate (and under-resource) the small things, which can be mighty.

underappreciate (and under-resource) the small things, which can be mighty. We leave changemaking in the hands of a few giants rather than vesting it in everyone.

We think that would be an ill-advised strategy. Stretching, as we'll see in Part III, is a re-enchantment with the small, with the everyday, with the seeming banality of daily interactions. Where innovation discourse centres on new things, or the new processes that give rise to the new things, our hunch is that the more people stretch toward a shared vision or outcome, the more we will see sustainable change.

7

No change without examining values

BEFORE OUTLINING SOME of the experiments that led us to the stretches we propose later in this book, we'd like to share a key take-away from our years of partnership: substantial change is possible only if we're willing to unearth the values and assumptions beneath our work and open them up to ongoing critique. If all we do is develop new solutions on top of the same foundation of values, we'll end up reproducing the same relationships, power dynamics, and staid outcomes. We won't be able to see the openings for change that exist at the root and branch level.

Values matter. True, many are rightly skeptical of the role that values play in organizations. It's easy to detect discrepancies between what we communicate in training and promotional materials and what we actually practice. We're all guilty of our rhetoric falling short of reality. But if that happens with any regularity, or with regular indifference, it becomes easy to view organizational values as empty platitudes, as things that are required by custom but are otherwise meaningless. Values are the weights that anchor our undertakings, whether we recognize them or not.

A common trap is to think that all we need to do is write down the value set for our work, then steadfastly uphold it. In fact, there is at all times a roiling sea of values, some rising to breach collective awareness, some remaining submerged in human interaction. All waiting for their moment, all having their place.

Permanently exalting or privileging only a handful of values can be dangerous. Take compassion. We rarely if ever question its role in the work we do. Compassion is at the root of caring and has made the social services possible. In a world that's often divided, compassion can melt away otherness, bind us together, and inspire us to act. But while compassion is a critical precondition for moral action, it's not enough on its own. We can do a lot of damage by not thinking through the ways in which compassion can inadvertently lessen others' sense of agency and choice. People in pain don't just need their experience validated, they need opportunities for esteem, love, belonging, and purpose. Compassion alerts us to moral problems, but it does little to lead us to meaningful solutions. Orphaned from other values like freedom and discernment, compassion can express itself in mawkish sentimentality, paternalism, even detrimental action. We have a long and uncomfortable history of harms caused by compassionate interference.

Empathy is another value worth examining, especially as it has become an in-vogue concept that goes hand in hand with social innovation and design thinking. With more empathy, the reasoning goes, we can unlock more human-centred solutions. But empathy by itself can't extract alternative possibilities from us, because we're limited by what we have seen and imagined. When we use empathy to design solutions to individual pain points, we can end up reinforcing root causes, preserving social structures and power dynamics, and leaving destructive assumptions uncontested. Empathy without critical analysis can be deeply problematic, and we'd argue that the social sector has an excess of the former and a shortage of the latter. We are operational problem solvers before we're critical thinkers; we are apologists before we're theorists or experimenters. While it's a good thing to continue fostering empathy, what we need most is more discernment, more learning, and more critical analysis.

Compassion and empathy are just two of the values that underpin our work. There are many, many more, and they are often in conflict. While these swirls of competing values call for moral discernment, the danger is that we will pluck out only a handful and choose to be continuously guided by them. This oversimplifies our duties to others and can lead to dogmatism—to blunting our moral sensibilities rather than sharpening them.

Being prepared to choose or create the values that make the most sense in a particular situation radically expands the field of what's possible for us to do or be—which can be scary, because we can't always depend on general rules or values to guide us. But being responsive in this way acknowledges and affirms that we are at all times in personal relation with others, and that we are free to choose how to be with them.

In times of adversity or constraint, we are forced to decide: what really matters? What's really important in this moment, to those we serve, to ourselves, and to the organizations we represent? If our organizational values offer only generic platitudes, we are left rudderless. At the same time, it can be better to be rudderless than to be cocksure. Navigating complexity and choosing wisely requires great humility. What are the alternatives to empty platitudes and unyielding ideology?

IF WE ARE to rethink our past and reimagine our future, we need to become a lot more conversant in values. That includes tracing their origins in our practices and circumscribing their limits.

Where are the safe spaces for this sort of research, reflection, and interrogation? And whom do we invite into those spaces? Contesting values and convictions is an important precondition to any change, but our systems are likely to proscribe such debate. As long as that's the case, we merely preserve the status quo and remain stuck.

It's not simply that we don't have time to reflect on core values, or that it's politically dangerous to question them (which it is). It's that there doesn't seem to be any good reason for unpacking them. They seem to make good sense. They are values that everyone appears to

Substantial change is possible only if we're willing to unearth the values and assumptions beneath our work and open them up to ongoing critique.

agree on; they're espoused by sectoral leaders and justified in pedagogy. They are the givens, whether in an orientation with a new employee or in a keynote presentation to executives. We accept them as basic to our work.

But we're in danger when we spend too much time brandishing values and not enough time reflecting on them. We're in danger when declaring values on a brochure or website is the end of our reflective work.

Innovation rarely inspects the beliefs and value sets behind either historical practices or the practices upon which innovative efforts are built. Innovation tends to proceed without an explicit ethical foundation, too often focused on coordination, efficiencies, and the exploitation of new technologies. This only increases the risk of extending the past, of shaping a future that doesn't fundamentally rethink what is good, for whom, when. For example, making an information-sharing app for social workers in the child protection system reinforces existing values around professional collaboration and efficiency. That's helpful for professionals, but not always helpful for individuals who may now have less say over who sees what information. An app on its own doesn't change the quality of the information collected, or who holds what kind of power, or the types of decisions that are made. If anything, it becomes one more system artifact that reinforces the way things are done.

We have all seen it: do-gooding confused with good-doing. That is why it's so important—if we want real, meaningful, lasting change—to be able to tease apart the convictions that drive our present-day systems, to excavate the historical assumptions that have gone into their construction, and to become clear about the sorts of values that we think might support the future of good work.

II

Three Phases
of Experiments

As the true method of knowledge is experiment, the true faculty of knowing must be the faculty which experiences. This faculty I treat of.

WILLIAM BLAKE

I N 2010, POSABILITIES (the organization Gord works for) launched an employment service for people with developmental disabilities. Our organization's role, we fervently believed, was to help people succeed in the community, and this new service aligned with that conviction.

The hitch was, there was no new money from government. If we wanted to set up the service, we'd have to reallocate internal resources. That meant persuading people we served to opt for the new employment service instead of their current offers, such as life skills and day programs. And that would be difficult. By and large, families preferred the security of a schedule of guaranteed services, and individuals were comfortable in those programs.

Our solution was to create a community connector role. If employment specialists could embed people with disabilities into a workplace, why couldn't we embed people into the community by finding them places to go, things to do, and people to do them with? Why couldn't we fill someone's schedule with activities outside of programs and services? Perhaps by combining the roles of community connector and employment specialist, we could get closer to the vision of people being genuinely part of community.

Three other organizations joined us: Kinsight, Burnaby Association for Community Inclusion, and Inclusion Powell River. Together we pooled our community connectors to create a single virtual storefront, Building Caring Communities, and a cadre of connectors who shared mentorship, theory, and practice.

Now, several years later, Building Caring Communities has gone through three theories of change, three evaluation systems, an in-the-field mentor, coaching from a social innovation guru, and training from InWithForward. And we're still trying to figure it out. We can report some good outcomes, and we've learned a lot, but we're still struggling to define the role and the practice. The work is incredibly complex because we often deal with individuals who have depression, anxiety, or motivational disinterest; with families who mistrust the community or understandably feel protective of their adult children; and with social stigma and other difficulties. Helping adults with intellectual disabilities become encircled by people in their neighbourhoods and communities is complicated.

This complication was partly what led to inviting InWithForward to come to British Columbia. We wanted to better understand the lived experience of social isolation and why it continued to increase even as people lamented it. We wanted to get smarter at brokering connectivity between diverse people, and we wanted to overcome stigma. We were hunting for something more rigorous, something we could visualize, translate, and share. Something that would finally begin to change the narrative of social isolation and loneliness for adults with intellectual disabilities.

8

Phase One: Projects, pilots, and prototypes

ONFRONTED WITH JUGGERNAUT problems like social isolation and stigma, and a historical inability to solve them, the Degrees of Change organizations aspired to come up with not only new solutions but new *categories* of solutions. We were dispirited by the sorts of initiatives being imagined inside our own sector, so we decided to look outside it for inspiration.

When InWithForward agreed to come work with Degrees of Change, things really ramped up. A recently vacated two-bedroom apartment, in a mid-rise complex managed by the Burnaby Association for Community Inclusion, seemed like the ideal blank canvas. On a rainy day in April 2014, the InWithForward team, newly arrived in Canada, rolled three suitcases up to the third floor and set up shop.

Apartment 303 became their living and work space. Sarah and designer Muryani bunked together. Lead designer Jonas Piet took the master bedroom, which would later double as our animation studio. We turned the living room into our design workshop, and with the help of IKEA shelving and jerry-rigged plastic tables, made room for three new team members: a Vancouver-based designer, a mid-level manager from posAbilities, and a community connector from

What if people's best years could be ahead of them, not behind them? What if conviviality wasn't a short-lived event but an ongoing experience?

Kinsight. We were a motley bunch—system insiders and system out-siders, locals and foreigners, analytic and creative types.

Our team had ninety days to chart out the space between the world as it was and the world as it could be. What were the everyday realities of our neighbours? What were their experiences of isolation and dis-connection? What might enable more people to thrive as part of their community? About twenty percent of our neighbours lived with intel-lectual disabilities, most of them supported by the Degrees of Change agencies. Going in, we thought these neighbours were socially iso-lated. Although they were physically housed in the community, they were living apart.

Days two through forty we spent masterminding new ways to get to know our neighbours. We turned the elevator into a giant colour-ing book, with Easter eggs dangling overhead, each egg containing an invitation to dinner. We offered breakfast in bed, chocolate ice cream on a bad day, and vacuum cleaner repairs. We started the day with a coffee cart in empty parking stalls and ended it with a door-to-door happy hour drink service.

It worked. We shared meals with fifty of our neighbours, swap-ping stories of the circuitous routes that landed us across the table from one another. We played homemade board games to explore con-cepts of home and belonging. We used magnetic poetry and decks of cards to probe how people saw themselves, their community, and their futures. We handed out disposable cameras along with activity prompts to see how young people construed their worlds. We went on walks with people to map their favourite spots. We accompanied our neighbours to the grocery store, the bank, and the pharmacy. We went to the pet shop to hold snakes and see how community members interacted. And we opened up our design workshop to late night chats and the occasional dance party.

Days forty-one through ninety saw us writing up stories from all this ethnographic design research. We harvested themes and gen-erated ideas to share back with our neighbours. We noticed that for residents with intellectual disabilities, one year kept coming up: 1986, the year the world's fair came to Vancouver. Expo 86 left an indelible mark on those who were around for the party. There were new people to meet, new foods to sample, new activities to try. All of this novelty seemed wrapped up in a warm, welcoming, convivial atmosphere. We wondered: what if people's best years could be ahead of them, not behind them? What if conviviality wasn't a short-lived event but an ongoing experience?

The thing about conviviality is that it emerges organically. It arises from authentic human connection and shared moments, not from convenience and expediency. Very few of our neighbours, including those with intellectual disabilities, were living solitary existences. They regularly came into contact with family members, other people with disabilities, and paid staff. It was the *quality* of those connections that we saw languishing. Many of our neighbours, particularly those with intellectual disabilities, kept having the same conversations on repeat. Their lives took on a *Groundhog Day* quality, reinforced by the uncontested assumption that people with intellectual disabilities need routine more than novelty. But without a source of novel experiences, like what Expo 86 provided, there were few conversation topics of mutual interest except the weather, the garden, and the barking dogs. In other words, people had little content with which to forge meaningful relationships, let alone to allow them to learn, grow, and aspire.

Over a two-day stretch, as spring slid into summer, we collaboratively came up with over thirty ways to lift the aspirational ceiling, bring novelty into the everyday, and spark more conviviality. We whittled down our ideas to the five most different. They included Nok Nok, a service to introduce neighbours to each other, and Coach in Your Corner, which offered a so-called wing-person to build lonely residents' confidence for dating and relationships. We tried to give all five ideas shape through role playing, stop-motion animation, and rapid live trials.

One idea, Kudoz, stood out for its breadth. Kudoz was an experience-sharing platform that would bring people together based on their passions and fascinations. Anybody could host experiences involving the things they loved—be it songwriting or stone carving— and people with disabilities could book those experiences in the same way you might book a car through a car-sharing app or rent a house

A new paradigm becomes a possibility only when others can see it, touch it, feel it, and compare it to the present.

through Airbnb. Not only might the platform address the problem of novelty, we thought, it could also bridge people to others in the community.

WHAT CHARACTERIZED THOSE first few months of partnership between InWithForward and Degrees of Change was our unfettered hopefulness and earnest anticipation. We let curiosity drive us, rather than expectations about results. There were no reporting requirements other than weekly debriefs, and no pre-set standards we had to perform to. InWithForward was new to the disability sector, so wholly unaware of its sacred cows. The Degrees of Change agencies were open to mostly anything because they knew the traditional approaches weren't going to work.

In the winter of 2015, after months of living together, InWithForward and Degrees of Change decided to go steady. Thankfully, the government funder was flexible, and the three Degrees of Change boards were willing to take a risk, so we took Kudoz from a sketch on paper into a small-scale prototype, just as we might construct the first version of a chair out of cardboard. InWithForward officially relocated from Europe to Canada, moving their design studio into a larger space within the Burnaby Association for Community Inclusion. We recruited the first thirty users: twenty community members and ten individuals with a disability. At that point, the Kudoz platform consisted of a basic website and a PowerPoint presentation rigged to function like an app.

As we were building our minimum viable product, we became acutely aware that our ambitions were growing. No single innovation would be the panacea. Kudoz, we realized, was only one response to the ingrained stagnation and stigma.

This realization is borne out in our data. Four years and nearly four hundred stories of change later, we continue to track and visualize how Kudoz builds capabilities, strengthens motivations, and creates fresh opportunities. Over seventy percent of the platform's active users report a significant change in their lives: how they see themselves and their future; their communication, transit, technology, and decision-making skills; and the places they go, the people they know, and the things they do. The Kudoz users who experience the biggest changes treat the platform as *one* tool. With the help of family or staff, these users leverage the interests they build and the connections they make for friendships, paid jobs, volunteer projects, and personal pursuits. And they do that in communities that are more primed for involvement. About half of the five hundred community members who have hosted experiences in the Kudoz catalogue have never before engaged with someone with a disability, which means we're catalyzing new resources for the disability sector.

Still, financing Kudoz remains a struggle. Fitting the platform back into a funding system that emphasizes health and safety and prioritizes those in crisis is very much like stuffing a square peg into a round hole. A core challenge is that Kudoz shapes *future* demand yet does little to relieve *current* demand. Our goal is to shift people's trajectories so they don't fall into formal services but instead are set up to lead good lives in convivial communities. Creating the right conditions for that requires dollars for roles and activities beyond service provision to people with disabilities. But direct service provision is a priority expenditure for people who are in crisis today. Preventing people from reaching crisis, in contrast, is a nice-to-have budgetary expenditure for a good year.

This thinking is understandable, if myopic. Yet for all the system incompatibility and funding uncertainty, we don't see any other choice except to keep creating future-focused services. A new paradigm becomes a possibility only when others can see it, touch it, feel it, and compare it to the present. Without a series of robust reference points, there's little hope of displacing current logics and demonstrating different values in action.

How, then, do we create those new reference points? Convincing organizations and funders to give us freer rein to develop them has not been easy. The paradox is this: if a solution is easy for a system to adopt or deliver, it tends to be either a reproduction of that system or a re-engineered likeness of it. By its very nature, a disruptive solution can't be easily implanted because it requires different conditions and nourishment.

Back in 2016, we felt the best way to move toward a new paradigm was to build the capacity of our organizations. Then we'd have more employees creating multiple solutions at once, resulting in more contributions to change at the root and branch level.

That turned out to be a naive hunch.

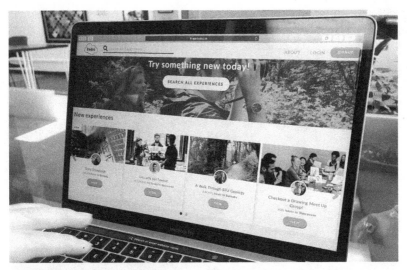

→ **TOP**: Launching app.kudoz.ca, an online booking platform, brokering adults with developmental disabilities to learning experiences offered by vetted community members *2018*.

→ **BOTTOM**: At Reflection Café, playing a board game designed to prompt intro-spection after a Kudoz experience, with Kudoz team member Andie Froese, Kudoz tester Sung Gyun, and community connector Megan Haliburton *2017*.

→ **ABOVE**: Working out the details of Grounded Space 1.0 and how to deepen Research & Development practice with Degrees of Change partners Richard Faucher, Fernando Coelho, Christine Scott, Heather Johnstone, Gareth Williams, Gord Tulloch, and InWithForward team members Sarah Schulman and Gayle Rice *March 2017.*

→ **OPPOSITE TOP**: Taking stock of our first year of Research & Development, with Degrees of Change partners Gord Tulloch, Tess Huntly, Fernando Coelho, Christine Scott, Tanya Sather, Richard Faucher, and InWithForward team members Sarah Schulman, Satsuko VanAntwerp, and Muryani *May 2015.*

→ **OPPOSITE BOTTOM**: Gathering in our living room/office to share the results of ten weeks of research on social isolation in a social housing complex, with Al Etmanski, Sabrina Dominguez, Vickie Cammack, Sarah Schulman, and Janey Roh *June 2014.*

→ **TOP LEFT**: Eric Stride and employment specialist Carla Mandy exploring character strengths with Kudoz coach Quinn Ashkenazy as part of a positive psychology coaching session *2018*.

→ **TOP RIGHT**: Kudoz curator Andie Froese working alongside a community member to design a new Kudoz experience about the Korean alphabet *2016*.

→ **BOTTOM LEFT**: Kudoz curator and host Andie Froese sharing her love of Mennonite history with Kudoer Larissa Gunkel *undated*.

→ **BOTTOM RIGHT**: Lindsey Aarstad building a birdhouse and learning how to safely use power tools as part of a Kudoz experience hosted by volunteer Jim Hobbs *September 2016*.

→ **ABOVE**: Testing community activation techniques, such as turning an elevator into a giant colouring book to meet neighbours, with InWithForward team members Jonas Piet and Sarah Schulman *April 2014*.

9

Phase Two: Building organizational capacity for R&D

THE SECOND PHASE of our experimentation started in 2016 with a seemingly logical assumption: if social service staff were trained in the research and design methods used to develop Kudoz, they too could understand the conditions of social problems, reframe those problems from the perspective of people on the ground, generate ideas, and test the impact and feasibility of their ideas. Then, instead of seeking out external, time-limited expertise, organizations could build internal capacity to come up with their own solutions.

Borrowing from the R&D practices of the technology sector, we introduced what's known as twenty percent time: one day a week dedicated to pursuing fledgling ideas. We called our experiment Fifth Space. We put out a call for thirty staff, ten from each Degrees of Change agency, to throw their hats in the ring. Some were staff who performed very well and were trusted by their organization. Some were the *un*usual suspects: staff whom managers might overlook, who didn't necessarily fit in with the establishment. We included a mix of directors, managers, supervisors, and front-line workers.

The emergent, unplanned nature of experimental practice consistently rubbed against people's need for clarity, structure, and defined timelines.

Every Tuesday for six months, those thirty staff crammed into a design studio and, with coaching from InWithForward's social scientists and designers, tried their hand at field research, data segmentation and analysis, problem definition, idea generation, storyboarding, rapid prototyping, and theories of change. Our hypothesis was that anybody could learn to ask critical questions and develop path-breaking concepts. We also thought we had built-in owners for any concepts that emerged: there would be far fewer orphan ideas because the ideas came from organizations with an appetite for change.

At the end of six months, we had six more branded solutions:

- Hire Wire, which bundled a series of small jobs with small businesses into part-time and full-time jobs for people with disabilities

- N'Tandem, an events-based platform that matched people with disabilities with new housemates and host families (inspired by speed dating and matchmaking algorithms)

- Check Mates, a weekly box of materials for front-line teams to use to build trust and reflective practice

- Share on Air, a podcast library of stories from individuals, families, and staff intended to help busy supervisors learn

- HackTivities, a platform whereby staff in group homes could earn praise and prizes for "hacking" day-to-day activities and making them more purposeful

- Ask a Dude, later rebranded as Real Talk, which supplied video content and honest conversations about sex, dating, and relationships (based on field research about adult men with disabilities thinking their sexuality is a source of shame)

Despite the promising prototypes, at the end of six months we faced burned-out staff, humbled coaches, and organizations that felt they'd just undergone a root canal. Not only did participants have jarringly different expectations about pace and communication, the public playbacks of the research and ideas also left the agencies feeling unfairly exposed and judged.

At the end of it all, despite the "proof" that we could surface promising and exciting new practices, leaders struggled to find the resources to advance them. Only Kudoz and Real Talk moved forward. Both had particularly entrepreneurial teams behind them that were able to source external funding.

Those who took part in Fifth Space described their twenty percent time as arduous and unsettling. Only a small cadre found the experience exhilarating. Where we had thought the lack of structure would be liberating, many found the wide parameters disorienting. The emergent, unplanned nature of experimental practice consistently rubbed against people's need for clarity, structure, and defined timelines. Staff in Fifth Space were accustomed to discussing and planning before taking action, which was antithetical to the rapid-fire iteration and prototyping we had hoped to inspire. Leaders of the organizations were often on the defensive, trying to calm nerves and smooth over last-minute course corrections.

At times, too, we were sloppy. Our design coaches were brand-new to the social services and needed more onboarding than we could provide. We were moving so quickly that communications were out of date by the time they got distributed. The schedule never seemed able to accommodate the latest, greatest ideas that someone had brainstormed overnight on the back of a napkin.

AT THE END of the six months, as staff returned to the rhythm of their jobs and reassumed their full slate of responsibilities, most hit a wall. They couldn't easily import the thinking and R&D they'd been exploring into their day-to-day structure. The design methods they had used—basically testing parbaked ideas with end users—challenged longstanding notions of managerialism. The informality of the methods—sketching, drawing, making early prototypes—challenged longstanding notions of professionalism. Even simple practices such

There is no training or incentive around knowing when to take risks, when to suspend policies or procedures, when to contest values, break rules, or hack one's role.

as visual note-taking and switching from sitting to standing meetings were seen as "too playful" or "gimmicky" to be taken seriously. New practices introduced new scripts, interfered with system flows and norms, and altered power dynamics, and were therefore met with natural resistance.

Rules of the game exist for good reason. Organizations are carefully balanced systems that require them. Systems naturally incentivize actions such as adhering to policies, procedures, and protocols; completing tasks; solving problems; and minimizing risk. Managers are trained to know these actions inside and out and to make sure they're enacted. There is no training or incentive around knowing when to take risks, when to suspend policies or procedures, when to contest values, break rules, or hack one's role, because those things can put everything at risk. Not only are these behaviours fundamentally discouraged, any employee who engages in them risks also being called out for flirting with danger, heresy, or insubordination.

Organizations talk about wanting their staff to show initiative. What they really mean is initiative that has a known and successful outcome. Even then, staff may not be rewarded. They may not even tell anyone for fear of getting in trouble. But when an employee goes off script and tries something different, and the outcome is less than ideal, the organization is likely to censure the individual for exercising poor judgement or ignoring processes installed to minimize the chance of things going wrong. That's why so many intrapreneurs try to fly under the radar and don't want to broadcast the creative things they're trying. Their experiments may not even be that creative, except insofar as they run counter to established rules or conventions. Routines at least supply predictable outcomes; creativity does not. And tepid outcomes are preferable to bad ones.

Once we saw how little the agencies were building new methods into their day-to-day practice, we revised our initial assumption. It wasn't a skills gap, we realized, so much as a cultural gap. Frontline staff and managers of social service agencies were stuck in a system that allowed for little lateral movement. Even if they picked up some R&D skills, they didn't have time to really develop or apply them, and it was difficult to exercise those skills in an environment that valued conservation—refining and consolidating existing practices and reducing errors. These were not the right conditions for experimentation.

If we wanted to re-choreograph the routines that these agencies followed, we would need to promote a culture in which the roles, expectations, and lines of authority embraced creativity. It was time to try to curate the conditions under which experimentation could occur. And so began the third phase of our partnership, Grounded Space.

Book

Talkback Video: Impact of Birth on Sexuality – Trina

How Do You Feel About Masturbation?

Have You Ever Wanted To Be Pregnant? Or To Prevent Pregnancy?

How Do You Support Your Partner and Show Them Love?

How Do You Know If Someone Is Attracted To You?

How Do You Know If Someone Is NOT Attracted To You?

→ **ABOVE:** Launching real-talk.org, with original video content showcasing adults living with developmental disabilities having honest conversations about sex, love, dating, and relationships *2018*.

→ **OPPOSITE TOP LEFT:** Richard Faucher and Christine Scott try out a Kudoz experience: learning about chickens from farmer Duncan Martin while Gord Tulloch and Sarah Schulman (in the background) learn how to make hollandaise sauce from a local chef *November 2014*.

→ **OPPOSITE TOP RIGHT:** Christine Scott testing an ethnographic tool with a neighbourhood mechanic *February 2015*.

→ **OPPOSITE BOTTOM:** Fifth Space members John Woods, Bobae Kim, Irena Flego, and Hayley Gray analyzing ethnographic research on perceptions of sex, dating, and relationships among adults with developmental disabilities *March 2015*.

10

Phase Three: Building an R&D culture inside organizations

GROUNDED SPACE kicked off in the spring of 2017, thanks to funding from two Canadian-based foundations: the McConnell Foundation and the Conconi Family Foundation. This time, rather than just transfer R&D *methods*, we'd try to build R&D *conditions*. We would set up design studios at each participating agency, carve out two new roles (including one for managers), and introduce habits that we hoped might become experimental business as usual. That's how we found ourselves adorning walls with chalkboard paint, getting rid of office furniture, moving in pillows and plants, and hanging indoor clotheslines.

Internally, we recruited for two new positions:

- Embedded researchers were staff who would be trained, supported, and given dedicated time to collect and act on new kinds of data. They would spend time in the field and on the front lines, paying attention to the lived experiences of individuals, families, and staff in order to reframe problems and find opportunities to experiment.

Instead of widening the space for R&D, the research pried open a nagging fear: that the conditions were mostly *wrong* for experimentation.

Later they would identify trends elsewhere in the world, select possible new practices, and test them out in collaboration with community.

- Culture curators were managers or senior leaders who would be coached to make space for experimentation. They would give staff permission to ask critical questions, share honest perspectives about the organization, and try new models of practice. They would also tell others about the purpose of Grounded Space, connect strategic dots, overcome roadblocks and tricky logistics, and help extract lessons learned.

By the fall of 2017, embedded research teams in all three Degrees of Change agencies had broken ground on their first task: identifying the organizational conditions for experimentation. Riffing on the behavioural change framework of health psychology professor Susan Michie, the teams spent time interviewing and observing staff to see what kind of capabilities, motivations, and opportunities the staff had to experiment with.

Six months later the teams were still in research mode, bogged down by the oh-so-normal realities of employee turnover and availability, scheduling conflicts, and ever-dwindling resources.

What emerged during our analysis wasn't all that surprising, but it was stark. Researchers zoomed in on five elements that shaped their staff's motivation, capability, and opportunity to try new things: (1) power and hierarchy, (2) roles and identity, (3) systems and processes, (4) values and beliefs, and (5) routines. Instead of widening the space for R&D, the research pried open a nagging fear: that the conditions were mostly *wrong* for experimentation. The social services were too firmly embedded in conservation, consolidation, and compliance for the teams to loosen.

Still, they tried. Each agency prototyped a solution:

- NewBe was a gamified orientation process for new staff at the Burnaby Association for Community Inclusion.

- Kea turned professional development into co-learning adventures between staff and people with disabilities at Kinsight.

- Meraki was a subscription box service designed to shake up routines and spark joy, creativity, courage, and human connection in day programs and group homes at posAbilities.

Focusing on organizational conditions, as we did, turned out to have a predictable result: the teams proposed organizational solutions, not user- or community-centric ones. Our hypothesis, or hope, was that if we began with an organizational pain point, such as staff ennui or autonomy, it would be easier to build the conditions for experimentation. Those conditions could then be leveraged to develop solutions with the people who used the services. But the grounds of our hope were dubious, and we knew it. Systems, and the people who make them up, are quite motivated to solve internal problems with insular fixes and improvements. While such fixes improve how a system functions, there's often little discernible benefit to the people it serves.

WE SAW, IN our third phase of experimentation, how easy it is for R&D to be co-opted for the purposes of continuous quality improvement. Excellence is a strongly held, motivating value in the social services, and R&D offers all kinds of promise for achieving it. But paradigm disruption is a different thing altogether from incremental improvement. The conditions that support internal quality improvement are unlikely to also support the contesting of system policies, processes, and roles, or the giving up of power and control.

We also realized that we had misstated our aspiration. Our goal was not simply to create the conditions for experimentation within organizations. Such a goal would be indifferent to purpose or ambition. What we were really after was flourishing lives for people. What we wanted were disruptive new practices that might collectively produce a new frontier for our sector. Instead, we were building a propensity for experimentation without any moral or visionary rudder. As a result, the ideas we got back reflected initial conditions, not aspirational ones.

So we tried a reset. Yes, we needed to respond to what wasn't working for staff, but it wasn't enough to simply spice up our problem solving with a little extra creativity. That wouldn't fundamentally change practices and norms. So we used the twelve stretches, introduced in Part III, as a filter for ranking our ideas along a continuum between "best" and "next" practices. After several more rounds of brainstorming and coaching, the agencies presented a more disruptive iteration of their ideas.

The posAbilities team, for instance, replaced their original concept of a digital idea-tracker (which, like UPS, would follow ideas from suggestion through approval or rejection and on to completion) with Meraki, a subscription box service that supplied do-it-yourself experiences for people with disabilities, their families, and workers. Meraki was less about increasing activities and more about inducing fresh mindsets and behaviours—like curiosity, social courage, and neighbourly connection—in staff and the people they supported. And because it needed to address barriers that might prevent the experience from happening, the new service came with all the necessary permissions and supplies. For example, a Community Crawl kit included permission for users to hack, wreck, adapt, or add to the box; some dog treats (so that staff wouldn't have to go out and buy them); and a prompt card to meet as many dogs and owners as possible. More recent versions of the boxed experiences experiment with topics that are often taboo, like sex and sexuality, and with content provided by local artisans, hobbyists, and entrepreneurs.

Part of Meraki's theory of change is that shifting norms and culture begins with micro-interactions. It involves gradually nudging people outside their comfort zones and reinforcing the movement with joy, connection, and learning. Even so, Meraki is still at the beginning of its journey as a prototype and is likely to undergo many more changes. Who knows where it will land?

Even with our pivot, we were all running out of steam, just as we had with Fifth Space during the second phase of our experimentation. The embedded researchers and culture curators we had recruited were depleted from the demands of their regular workloads plus participating in Grounded Space. InWithForward was exhausted from work weeks that didn't stop in the evenings or weekends. Everyone felt beleaguered, and the excitement that had launched and sustained this effort had largely fled.

Of the ideas produced during our third phase, only Meraki would move forward, thanks to an infusion of external grant dollars from the Vancouver Foundation.

ALL THAT SCRAMBLING was wearying, and in our collective exhaustion, trust wore thin. The Degrees of Change partners weren't sure that InWithForward really appreciated the challenges of their context, and InWithForward wasn't sure that the partners were as audacious as they needed to be.

More fundamentally, we had to ask: what was the scrambling for? We were no longer convinced it was possible to build the culture or the capacity for disruption within the social services. The more we tried to understand organizational contexts, and to design alongside the existing stakeholders, the more we found ourselves encumbered by the sector's preoccupations and conventions. Ideas were drowning in incrementalism instead of breaking new ground. And they tended to become more technocratic, not more human.

It's not that we stopped believing the social services could or would change. Rather, we began to think that, when it came to R&D, the opportunity wasn't so much *inside* organizations as it was at *arm's-length* from them—offsite and with more control over its own decisions and rhythms. More often, opportunity was between these arm's-length experiments and community, because showing up differently opened up new ways of connecting, relating, and collaborating. Rather than expecting staff to lead experiments, maybe we needed to catalyze a much broader set of actors—individuals, families, community members, spiritual leaders, and business owners—and situate new prototypes in the space between. Some of the most interesting and inspiring cases that we were coming across were happening outside social service organizations, at the hands of people like convenience

Reimagining the social welfare state is not about simply retooling the system, but about involving community in its broadest sense.

store owners and security guards who had no systems to constrain their goodwill or shape their intention. For such individuals, there is little distinction between will and action, between thinking and doing.

Five years of trying to reshape the social service system and coming up against its inherent stickiness began to confirm our previous instincts that reimagining the social welfare state is not about simply retooling the system, but about involving community in its broadest sense. It was not about simply invigorating statutory frameworks and increasing access to services, but about co-constructing communities that bring about better lives for everyone.

The most inventive solutions, we have come to believe, are the ones that will recast relationships between multiple actors, resetting the social contract rather than merely readjusting organizational dynamics. It is this realization that has led us to our fourth and *in progress* phase, Grounded Space 2.0.

→ **TOP LEFT**: Grounded Space 1.0 crew members from posAbilities making sense of interview data with front-line staff from across the agency *November 2017.*

→ **TOP RIGHT**: posAbilities staff and Grounded Space 1.0 crew members learning how to use behaviour change theory to explain experimental behaviour *November 2017.*

→ **BOTTOM LEFT**: Grounded Space 1.0 crew members from the Burnaby Association for Community Inclusion and posAbilities testing how to segment end users to find patterns and surface insights *February 2018.*

→ **BOTTOM RIGHT**: Grounded Space 1.0 crew members from the Burnaby Association for Community Inclusion building a theory of change for their prototype of a new kind of staff onboarding *May 2018.*

→ **ABOVE**: Asia Hollingsworth and Sherri Crane, Grounded Space 1.0 crew members from posAbilities, making a physical model of an idea to bring novelty and surprise to front-line staff *May 2018.*

→ **OPPOSITE TOP**: Kinsight Embedded Researchers Julian Avelino, Angela Kim, and Michelle Mastrandrea record a short film from the year 2030 as part of a generative exercise on the future of disability services *May 2018.*

→ **OPPOSITE BOTTOM**: An early prototype of Meraki at a day program, with posAbilities staff Lars Moberg *June 2018.*

meraki

Sam's box

Shauna's box

James' box

Andie's box

Josey's box

Janna's box

Mel's box

Steph's Box

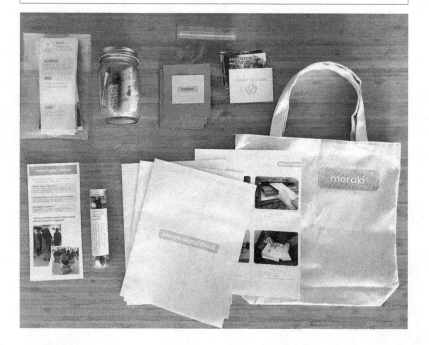

→ **ABOVE**: Hosting a co-design picnic in the park with newcomers in Surrey to solicit feedback on five concepts to change the newcomer experience with Options Community Services *August 2019.*

→ **OPPOSITE TOP**: A first iteration of the Meraki website, showcasing the first season of subscription box content, each version crafted with the help of a community member muse.

→ **OPPOSITE BOTTOM**: A choice-making kit as part of Meraki, designed to help front-line workers in group homes and disability day programs introduce box choice *November 2019.*

11

Recovering tensions

OF THE MANY lessons we learned over the past five years, the most enduring—and the one that permeates this book— has been how to live with tension, both personally and organizationally.

To be human is to experience ourselves as a contradiction, as divided and conflicted. We have contrary drives, values, needs, behaviours, and beliefs. Our contradictory nature is a feature of being human, and authenticity requires us to come to terms with it rather than suppressing parts of ourselves so that we project a coherent (but counterfeit) notion of self. It's the tensions and paradoxes we experience that give rise to possibilities, which in turn give birth to human freedom.

Designing a world that doesn't yet exist, as we were trying to do, asks that we understand and work with, rather than against, our own internal conflicts and contradictions. As we keep relearning, it isn't easy to experience ourselves this way. We naturally resist.

Systems are similar: they dislike being pulled in two directions at once. And this internal struggle is only exacerbated when it's externalized between people trying to establish a common purpose and path. We don't want our collective undertakings to be characterized by struggles and confusion. It's distressing when our values or concepts

When we cling to
notions of who is most
right, or assume that
our frame of reference
is most right, we risk
stepping into destructive
forms of conflict.

conflict, because it makes the path forward less obvious, our purposes less clear, and our teams more polarized. That's why systems have a penchant for "curing" tensions. Tensions are typically seen as problems that need to be resolved, as forks in the road that we must choose between, or as distractions to be ignored because they produce angst to no practical effect.

One of the most important tensions in human organizations is the pull between order and disorder (this is the basis of chaordic design, a concept introduced by Dee Hock in 1999). Too much order or control limits creativity and learning; too much disorder produces waste and instability. Organizations have a bias toward more order rather than less. We see this in their endless development of standards and processes, in their attempts to increase clarity around roles, reporting, training, expectations, and so on. The risk of this predilection is that the environment in which organizations operate becomes more and more cluttered with structure. We see more of the obstacles that we kept encountering during our experiments: top-heavy systems; obstructions to creativity, autonomy, and growth; a culture of compliance. It's critical, for organizations to function optimally, that some things *not* be pinned down. We need some ambiguity. Disorder plays an important role, and so does the absence of structure. Without them, human action and creativity become impossible, and there's only room for imitation.

The same can be said for truth. Systems struggle to hold multiple truths at once. Managers are expected to look at information objectively, draw conclusions about what and who is most right, and take corrective action. There's little time or space to probe what lies behind the perspectives at play, or to explore what makes "right" right in the first place.

When we cling to notions of who is most right, or assume that our frame of reference is most right, we risk stepping into destructive forms of conflict. We end up choosing hierarchy to resolve tensions. When we do that, we not only drain our pool of trust and goodwill, we also lose the opportunity to identify shared needs and frustrations. We lose the opportunity to come up with relational (rather than managerial) solutions—solutions that involve new kinds of interactions between people rather than simply progressive discipline or more training.

What we found, after five years of trial and error, is that it's the tensions that exist between polarities—whether we're talking about our focuses, roles, frameworks, or values—that provide the most fertile spaces for creativity and inventiveness.

We see the core challenge for social service systems as this: can they become sophisticated enough to preserve and explore those tensions rather than collapse them? Can they restore a balance between important and useful concepts where historical or contemporary prejudice has impugned them? Can they walk a path between polarities rather than instinctively elevating one over the other? And can they avoid trying to immediately colonize the space that opens up once a tension is allowed to remain?

III

Twelve Stretches

Possibility is not a luxury;
it is as crucial as bread.

JUDITH BUTLER

JIM WAS A down-to-earth guy. He worked in construction during the day, hiked on weekends, and enjoyed craft brews with friends. Every few months, as a Kudoz host, he would drive his pickup to a parking lot in Burnaby, British Columbia, take out his tools, and build birdhouses, an activity he did along with people with disabilities who shared his passion for carpentry.

Jim was a local resource. And he wasn't alone. Sammy, a convenience store owner in Edmonton, kept his doors open twenty-four hours a day to give people living on the streets a warm place to go, a smile, and a listening ear. Donna, the office manager at a private health clinic on the east side of Vancouver, called lonely seniors to have a nice chat.

Jim, Sammy, and Donna had no formal role in the social welfare state, but their interactions with people point toward a renewed social contract—one based not on charity or obligation but on mutuality and reciprocity; one that involves informal bonds, not just formal programs; one built around people and community and heart, not systems and frameworks.

The question isn't just *how* our future social service models tap into the Jims, the Sammys, and the Donnas, but *why* they tap into them. Birdhouses, smiles, and chats are not soup and sandwiches—they're not instruments of survival. They are instruments of love, connection, meaning, and purpose. They are instruments of humanity.

12

Stretching our focuses

O VER THE PAST five years, as we (and our organizations) have trekked toward a new model for the social services, climbing forward a ways and often stumbling back, the vision of flourishing lives has been our joint North Star. Together we've sought to clarify the vision, to make it real and practicable and actionable. The only way to do this, we believe, is to embrace the tensions and polarities that are an inescapable part of human relationships and the systems that grow up around them. Accepting tensions, and restoring the space between them, is the essence of what we call our stretch approach.

Taking a stretch approach, as you'll see in the twelve stretches we propose below, is not about abandoning one "right" way for a new and better way. It's not about a shift, exactly. Instead, it's about extending ourselves so that we inhabit additional space. It's about increasing our mental, ethical, and operational agility. It's about avoiding contraction.

And it implies discomfort. There's no question—tensions are uncomfortable. The unwillingness to suffer tensions is one reason we see so many pendulum swings. Because we can't easily occupy the space in between, we veer from pole to pole. Yet we have found that when we take our place *within* tension, that's where complexity is best understood and honoured, where creativity and opportunity become possible, and where equilibrium is restored.

To stretch, as we hope to show you, is to move through the sticking points. It means resisting the seduction of "either/or," which radically shrinks our field of vision, and attending to "both/and," which offers almost limitless conceptual and opportunity space between poles.

In the twelve stretches that follow, we will articulate the principles that are now guiding us, sometimes explicitly and sometimes implicitly, and share with you the learning we've accumulated along the way. These are twelve stretches that we think are critically needed in serving people with intellectual disabilities, at the very least. Might they also apply to your sector of the social service world? We invite you to reflect on that as you read.

Each stretch we explore begins with a word pair. The first term in the pair refers to an important function or competence already supplied within the social service system. We're not challenging these functions or suggesting that we stop doing them. Rather, we propose a second term that brings additional functionality, capacity, and purpose, and that requires us to pull in new directions. Because we aren't dismissing the first term, the second, when added, will introduce operational tensions. By allowing both terms to exist side by side, we hope to benefit not only from the wisdom inherent in each, but from the extensive space between the two. It's in that space where we, and you, can contemplate action.

Consider these twelve stretches a manifesto, if you like—or an anti-manifesto, since we're cautious of any ideology holding court. For our organizations, the stretches will frame our future strategic thinking and help us decide where to invest our resources and energies. If any of the stretches resonate with you, or if you have examples of what they look like, please join our online community and explore with us different ways to apply them. Perhaps if we work collectively, we can reimagine and unstick the social services flotilla we're a part of.

What self do we want to become? The answer to that question is partially contained in the answer to a different question: "What self do we allow others to become?"

THE PRESENT-DAY SOCIAL service system is largely the result of focusing on needs that we can see: conditions like hunger, homelessness, and illness. And yet we know that the needs we cannot see—interior conditions such as purposelessness, loneliness, and shame—are equally profound.

How do we stretch so that we can engage with the soul? How do we encounter the person rather than the service recipient? How do we speak spirit? If we cannot navigate these deeper currents, we will remain stuck in the shallowest parts of the stream.

1 Safety ☼ Flourishing

FAY'S APARTMENT WAS on the ground floor. On the door was a handwritten sign asking people to knock. Visitors were welcome—with notice.

Anyone who walked through Fay's kitchen to the living room would see two clear motifs: dogs and Disney. For Fay, owning a dog was the epitome of independence because it meant being responsible for another living being. Growing up in an institution, she had little control over how she spent her time and with whom. Now her dog Rocco set the pace of her days and was the subject of many of her conversations. The rest of her conversational repertoire mostly involved her frequent medical appointments and health issues.

Despite living on her own for more than a decade, Fay lived a highly routinized life. She saw a life skills worker a couple of days a week, and every night a nurse dropped by to prepare her for bed.

STRETCHING OUR FOCUSES   121

Although Fay wanted more in her life, when asked what she would do if money were no issue, she said, "Dinner and a movie." When asked again, this time reminded that she could ask for anything, she said, "Dinner at the Old Spaghetti Factory." That was the only restaurant Fay knew. It was her birthday treat every year.

SOCIAL SERVICES TRY to keep people as safe as possible. It's an objective that ongoingly informs training, policies and procedures, and monitoring practices.

But no matter how we define a good life, safety isn't enough. Nor is just getting by. How do we help people flourish and to thrive? How do we help them lead full lives—connected to others, participating in community life, and remaining resilient? Instead of just catching people in our safety nets, how can we become trampolines that launch them into full and meaningful lives? How do services become conduits to the good life, rather than offering perpetual harbour?

Financial poverty significantly restricts flourishing and it is past time to confront the structural inequalities that so egregiously limit opportunity. At the same time, there are also other forms of poverty which we haven't paid much attention to that can similarly shrink opportunity. Chief among these is a poverty of experience.

Part of flourishing requires that there be a rich supply of experiences. Experiences shape our thoughts, desires, and possibilities. The fewer experiences we have, and the less we can imagine for ourselves or think about, the less there is to motivate and inspire us and the less the self can grow and develop. Without experience, we're unable to refine our understanding of the world or ourselves, our sense of opportunity, purpose, and being.

It's not enough, therefore, to offer choices or person-centred planning to someone like Fay, who hasn't had much breadth of experience. When we do that, we run the risk of consigning an individual to an endless cycle of limited (and limiting) experiences—like trips to the mall or park, like bowling or movies, like dinners at the Old Spaghetti

A ship in harbor is safe, but that is not what ships are built for.

JOHN A. SHEDD

Factory. It's not that these activities are "bad"—they're a part of our lives too—but we also have milestones such as graduation, promotions, marriages, and kids alongside the activities.

If we overlook developmental progress, banal activities can systemically degrade people's potential rather than complement or actualize it. Our first duty is to stretch what we offer: to provide robust exposure to varied and novel experiences that stretch people's horizons. Only then can we ask someone what they want to do or who they want to be.

There is also poverty of expectations. When we don't see in others the potential for growth and contribution, for reasoning and creativity, or for personal agency, we become oriented toward preservation instead of aspiration. We reinforce stigma about what is and must be the case, rather than attending to who one might become. We take over more, decide more, speak more—and the subjects of our services become ever-dwindling footnotes in their own lives. With this growing existential inertia comes a spiral into anxiety, hopelessness, and despair. And, probably, the need for more services.

It is long past time to rethink risk and vulnerability. Our efforts to minimize or contain these threats can thwart opportunities for those in our care. Living an unfulfilled life carries a greater risk of harm than what may befall someone in the pursuit of their dreams. The latter can be folded into a story; the former is the absence of story. The latter is a movement toward possibility; the former is the disintegration of it. But so long as organizations and governments are the sole owners of risk, and so long as vulnerability is regarded as a pathology instead of a human condition, we're at risk of exchanging good lives for safe but artificial ones. As Søren Kierkegaard wrote in *The Sickness Unto Death*, "The greatest danger, that of losing one's own self, may pass off as quietly as if it were nothing; every other loss, that of an arm, a leg, five dollars, a wife, etc., is sure to be noticed."

We cannot allow that kind of loss to happen to the people in our care. We must be vigilant because their very selves are at stake. As are our own. The self that we inhabit is determined in large part by our interactions with others and the nature of our influence on them. Are we a springboard for others or do we overprotect others in the name of their own safety and, perhaps especially, our own? Are we aiding in the development and unfolding of their being, or are we soothers, skeptics, or guardians? What self do we want to become? The answer to that question is partially contained in the answer to a different question: "What self do we allow others to become?"

As we look to the future, we need to recognize that vulnerability is an essential feature of human life: of the people we support, our employees, our neighbourhoods, ourselves. It's not something to overcome but something to embrace. It's what makes trust and resilience intelligible, and what makes acts of care and cooperation possible.

Stretch questions

- How do we rework accountability frameworks so that they're informed by deeper philosophical and psychological conceptions of human needs and striving?

- How do we use vulnerability as a force of social change rather than as a worrisome susceptibility that emphasizes that people are unsafe?

- How do we distribute risk so that it's shared, not only by employees, organizations, and governments, but also by individuals, circles, and communities?

2 Body ⟳ Soul

THE IDACTION MOBILE project, conceived of and run by Exeko, an organization in Montreal, features a van that tours shelters, prisons, Indigenous communities, and the downtown core in order to reach out to the disenfranchised and homeless, especially young people and Indigenous peoples. The team doesn't include any social workers, homeless workers, or youth workers, nor does it provide food, clothing, or other familiar kinds of outreach. Instead, the team consists of philosophers, circus performers, and artists who distribute books, magazines, art supplies, journals, and conversation. Their express purpose is to nourish the soul through creativity and reflection.

Sometimes the team uses artist portraits and self-portraits to provoke a conversation about the role of appearances in society. In the middle of just such a conversation (during which Pierre Duchesne, then lieutenant governor of Quebec, and his wife, Ginette Lamoureux, dropped by), the room was invited to ask questions. One participant asked, "What is homelessness?" A rich discussion ensued. Someone argued that society makes people homeless, and that without social regard and financial means, one can do nothing. Olivier, another participant, disagreed: "Before, I thought that poverty was monetary. But the worst is not the lack of money, it is the poverty of the body and the spirit."

There is nothing in the world, I venture
to say, that would so effectively help one
to survive even the worst conditions, as
the knowledge that there is a meaning
in one's life.

VIKTOR FRANKL

THE SOCIAL SERVICES typically focus on physical needs such as shelter, income, clothing, and food. These basics are important, and they supply some of the preconditions that can result in change, but they do not have the power themselves to change lives. They don't result in a good life, either—at least, not by themselves.

The axes of change are things like beauty, meaning, purpose, love, reflection, laughter, and hope. These are not extras or add-ons. They are essential, fundamental. They make life worth living and transformation possible. The summons to live fully cannot be answered with food or shelter alone. Those provisions are the fulcrums of survival, not living. What do they matter when hope ceases to exist, when one's sense of worthiness is extinguished, when beauty has drained out of the everyday? When life is but a process of dying?

Where has spirit gone in the social services? For too long we have suppressed words of spirit and restricted our speech to the lifeless jargon of our professions. But longing for the sacred, for a greater wholeness, is part of our human inheritance.

While it's not our business to become envoys of religious leaders or mystics, of naturalists or spiritualists, it is our business to stretch beyond the physical needs of the people we work with and pay attention to the deep-seated impulse, which we all share, to understand our part in a greater story. In the end, perhaps there's little difference between a poet and a theologian, or between a song, a meditation, and a prayer. Our task is to learn to speak to people's spirit, however it asks to be spoken to. If we choose to pursue social change without appealing to what is mysterious or sacred, our efforts will be greatly enfeebled.

What are the dimensions of a life worth living? That's a question to be explored with people individually because it is a deeply personal affair. The inner world of some may expand through the arts, humanities, and philosophy—through exposure to literature, music, poetry, and lore. Others may be stirred by science or technology, or comedy, or political action, or surrendering to the Great Mystery.

We discover ourselves in the story of the world; we discover the world by coming to terms with ourselves. What is a self—myself—in the great unfolding of the universe? This monumental question is fundamentally about mattering. It's about having purpose. It's about answering the universal and specific summons to live.

Stretch questions

- How do we address purpose and beauty through our work, and present opportunities to reflect on existence and the individual's place in it?

- How do we change our conversations so that they're not just about program curricula, activities, or goals, but also about the stuff of life? How might the two come closer together?

- How do we invite spirit or mana back into our institutions and create a protected place for it?

3   Behaviour 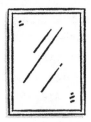 Identity

WHEN OUR TEAM moved into that mid-rise housing complex in Burnaby, back in 2014, we set out to understand who the residents were and what they wanted from their lives. What were their motivations, values, and dreams?

Trying to elicit this information from residents with intellectual disabilities proved challenging. We tried several approaches, including prompts such as homemade games and card sets with pictures and labels, but it remained a struggle to understand how people living with disabilities saw themselves, what made them tick, and what was important to them.

What consistently percolated up were people's descriptions of themselves as problems and deficits. They talked about what they couldn't do, what they were bad at, what they needed help with. It was profoundly unsettling. Where were the stories of yearning and striving, of milestones accomplished and crossroads ahead? Where was the "I" beyond that of service recipient? The existential harm hinted at in their responses was too distressing to think about.

To make matters worse, most people didn't know the nature of their disability. They hadn't been given a chance to learn about it and fold it into a healthy, strong sense of self. Not only had our agencies failed to work on the "story of them" with these residents, but the only story they had internalized was the story of their inadequacies. And that came from the service system.

IN THE WORK we do, much of our focus is on visible things, on people's bodies and behaviours. This is true not only of our interactions with the people we support, but also of our employees and organizational processes—we attend to their behaviours, goals, tasks, activities, procedures, training, skills, scheduling, reporting, planning, and so on. In pursuing important goals, such as predictable results, we focus on what we can see and tweak, so much so that we're becoming more enamoured of quantitative design methods over qualitative ones, and we're embracing the austerity of randomized control trials to demonstrate effects.

We would argue that when it comes to having lasting impact, more fundamental than learning discrete bits of demonstrable knowledge, skills, and behaviours is a sense of self and identity. *Who am I?* How a person answers this question can determine so much. The stories that make up "me" determine what is possible or impossible, desirable or undesirable. They provide the meaning that compels us throughout our lives, that justifies and condemns, that helps us make sense of the world around us. These stories distinguish who we are from who we aren't, and tell us who we can or cannot become. When the answer to the rudimentary question *Who am I?* changes, new worlds and possibilities open up. New ways of being, imagining, and relating present themselves. Changing the story of me changes the future of me.

We mustn't be so naive as to think that changing stories is about simply speaking new words. Words are embodied things; they are constrained by the limits and possibilities of our biology, our understanding, our personality, our psychological tendencies. Sometimes changing the story is about wresting our story and meanings back from others. Sometimes it's about self-discovery and trying on new language or meanings to see what fits. And sometimes it's about choosing to perform differently, think differently, and show up differently.

It is hard work. Identity isn't readily changed, and the possibilities aren't endless. There will be limits to our plasticity. Where identity is concerned, our language and imagination push up, our bodies and formative experiences push down, and the way others see us push in. Somewhere in that crucible of forces the self is formed.

Those who do not have the power over the story that dominates their lives, the power to retell it, rethink it, deconstruct it, joke about it, and change it as times change, truly are powerless, because they cannot think new thoughts.

SALMAN RUSHDIE

Program goals and activities, at least as they're presently conceived and operated, do not supply nourishing ground on which identity can form, and they are unlikely to produce the kinds of stretches toward identity that will improve life trajectories. Identity has little to do with a checklist on a form, after all. Nor is it a matter of adding Indigenous art to a wall, curry to a menu, or taking someone to church on Sunday (though all those things may be relevant). It's about how you take your place in history—how you understand your past and how you step into your future. It's about forming and unforming beliefs and convictions. It's about how you understand and describe your needs, dispositions, values, and ambitions.

People's stories of who they are carry power. Not only should we pay attention to these stories, we also should foster the conditions in which constructive identities can form and take root. Until we get better at talking about and engaging at the level of identity, it will be impossible to reach the heart or spirit or soul. We will continue to treat bodies and behaviours, but not the meaning(s) that animate them. Deeper and more enduring change will elude us.

Stretch questions

- How has our involvement in the lives of those we support positively and negatively influenced their identities? What stories have they internalized?

- How do we introduce new scripts, language, and imagery that might enable people to adopt more constructive and healthier views of themselves and their place in the world?

- How do we address deep emotions like shame, helplessness, and inadequacy and cultivate new narratives to overcome them?

4   Individuals ⟲ Circles

MARTHA WAS SURPRISED at the knock on her door. She wasn't expecting company. On the other side stood a jovial-looking guy named Sean, with a wrapped present in his hands. It was her son CJ's birthday, but no one except family had been invited to celebrate. CJ didn't have friends, Martha thought. For years he'd been bullied at school and had grown quiet and withdrawn at home. While they'd given him a cell phone, Martha didn't see much evidence that he knew how to use it.

She called CJ over to the door, then watched as the two exchanged big smiles. CJ, she realized, not only had a friend but was using his phone to communicate with him. The pair had met on a Kudoz experience. Sean was a photography host, which probably explained CJ's newfound interest in hiking and landscapes.

As Martha listened to Sean and CJ banter in the living room over cake, a feeling of immense happiness washed over her. Yet it was tinged with sadness. CJ had a clear ability to connect, but part of her had stopped believing it was possible. Now, watching her son interact sparked a buried hope and a forgotten optimism. If CJ could build relationships, what else might be possible?

PROGRAMS AND SERVICES for adults tend to centre on the individual. Organizations often struggle to meaningfully involve members of the individual's larger circles, whether they're families, friends, neighbours, or acquaintances. Yet we know that people's circles play crucial roles. The nature and extent of their involvement determines what will be possible. People generally perform to the standards and expectations that are foisted on them. Do others have high or low expectations for their ability to live a full and purposeful life? Are they perceived as capable or incapable? Can they make their own decisions? Are they provided with a nurturing environment, one that helps them learn and grow? Do their circles lift them up and nudge them forward, or do they hold them back?

Skills-based programs can't just teach individuals; there have to be opportunities in individuals' everyday lives to rise to those expectations and to use those skills. Getting into life isn't about spending years in mock environments until you pass enough tests. It's about

I love the idea that it doesn't take one person only to achieve your potential. It takes a village, it takes a community, a street, a teacher, a mother.

MIRA NAIR

wading into life's richness and complexity, just like everyone else, and reaching out for help when you need it, just like everyone else. If we want people to succeed in life, we need to stretch our attention to include the others who play important roles in their lives, and we need to figure out how to respectfully engage those others, how to support them and honour them. Our employees are amazing people, but they are poor surrogates for family members, neighbours, or employers. They can't supply through programs what those others supply out in the world where life is lived.

In recent initiatives that we've been involved in, such as the Kudoz platform, the critical role of family has come into even sharper focus. In cases where parents saw the growth potential in their adult child with an intellectual disability, where they were supportive of that person taking risks and making independent decisions, where they were willing to trust in the goodwill of community, we saw greater gains. In cases where these factors were missing, the results were too often flat.

We, as social service providers, are only one touchstone in someone's day or week. We can coach, empower, nudge, teach, and encourage people, but if those around them aren't similarly oriented, it's unlikely that much will change. And if we arrogantly presume that it's our programs and services that deliver meaningful outcomes, we will eventually be unmasked as fools and frauds. It takes a village.

Some of those we support have little to no family, friends, or acquaintances beyond our employees. Disconnected lives tear at our social resilience. When we don't know or care for each other, our collective capacity to respond to threats and opportunities is significantly weakened. We think agencies can play a role in strengthening the social fabric.

The everyday work that we do, no matter how good, is destined to be temporary and demoralizing if it can't be sustained in people's lives outside of programs and services. Beyond working with individuals, we need to engage circles; beyond being person-centric, we must also be network-centric.

Stretch questions

- How do we engage circles (family, friends, neighbours) without (further) disempowering individuals?

- Circle members face struggles in their own lives—how do we apply resources differently so that we can address everyone's wellness?

- How do we build the resilience of the entire network and not simply enlist their support?

13

Stretching our roles

A S WE'VE THOUGHT about the roles that we and others play within the social services, we've found ourselves asking two questions.

The first question is general: what role do social service organizations have in reimagining and repurposing the social welfare system? Even though they are vestigial products of certain histories, we think organizations play a critical part. They operate on the ground with people, where moral obligations are more visceral than notional, and they offer extensive social infrastructure. The challenge is to co-create a shared new vision, and to spread it.

The second question is much more specific: what sorts of roles can deliver these reimagined focuses? The roles may be listed separately on an organizational chart or may be part of broader job descriptions. In our experience, the latter tends to be less effective because the new functions must compete with other priorities.

We expect that many new roles will need to be invented, roles that reside inside and outside organizations. Here are just three that we think will be of critical importance.

5 Helpers ⟳ Brokers

AT FIRST GLANCE, the Thornhill family seemed like any other. Mom and Dad worked in a grocery store, and their two sons took computer classes at the local college. Yet the Thornhills were remarkable because they had quietly figured out, through ingenuity and trial and error, something that had eluded the adult disability system: how to reduce the cost of care and improve outcomes.

Both of the Thornhill sons had a diagnosis of autism. And both had a deep-seated passion for computer programming and animation. Rather than secure assistance for their sons based on their disability, the Thornhills wondered if they could somehow get peers involved based on their boys' shared interests. They turned down formal programs and services and, after applying for a moderate amount of funding, turned instead to Craigslist. They posted an ad directed at students in computer programming and animation who would be open to providing their boys with some practical help. They could all geek out together, go to classes, do homework, and hang out. And because they knew that it's ultimately people who keep people safe, not systems, the parents felt that their sons would be fine.

The Thornhills did not go with an expensive (and probably unsatisfying) service solution. Instead, they brokered connections that made natural sense. They tapped into a resource—the student body—that was ready and willing to be activated, and that met everyone's needs. In the language of social sciences, the Thornhills would be considered positive deviants: families who have found their own solutions to challenging circumstances.

The degree to which I can create relationships which facilitate the growth of others as separate persons is a measure of the growth I have achieved in myself.

CARL ROGERS

FAMILIES LIKE THE Thornhills have much to teach us as we reimagine service deliverers as brokers, not just helpers who provide care.

We sometimes think of the adult disability sector as a giant planet with its own density and mass. As soon as people come into its orbit, an inexorable tug pulls them deeper into services. Why does this happen? There are many reasons. People are usually eligible for our services because of chronic issues, not acute ones; a deficit-based system can always identify more needs to address; our sector has reinforced the perception that only trained professionals are qualified to provide support; system accountabilities tend to result in a tighter grip, not a looser one; we focus on stabilizing, maintaining, and supporting, not increasing and actuating possibilities; we work very hard for people to be happy with what we offer so that they want to stay with us; and people expect to get the services that have been "promised" to them—though that is beginning to change, perhaps.

Whatever the reason, people rarely bounce out of our services. They tend to sink deeper into them. There is a deeply custodial streak to our work, a kind of protectiveness and taking-care-of. People are vulnerable, so we encircle them. The world is unjust and ignorant, so we create safe, supportive environments. It's easy to simply give someone what the world hasn't readily supplied. It makes us feel better, because we care deeply about those we support and we want to show them a reality where they matter, where they have some modicum of power, where they are safe to be themselves. But it can be a poisoned gift.

Accreditation surveyors sometimes ask themselves in the field, "Would I recommend this service for a family member?" It's surprising that the question isn't, "Would I want this service for myself?" How many of us could endure settling for a surrogate world when we know there is so much more? And if we can't imagine that world for ourselves, if we feel it would rob us of life, why do we feel good about creating such an environment for others?

There's nothing wrong with giving help unless it fundamentally interferes with someone's self-realization and constrains their potential. Our role, we believe, is to channel people through our services so that they become part of community life to the greatest extent possible. Our role is to stretch beyond giving help and instead connect people with a life outside of programs and services—with meaningful jobs, friends, activities, and places where they experience belonging.

To do this, we need more brokers—employees who can forge community connections and relationships, and who can comfortably navigate diversity, engage strangers, and bridge people to new experiences and opportunities in the community. People who inhabit broker roles speak the language of reciprocity; they may not know the language of social services at all. They love people and diversity and the vision of a caring, cooperative society. Brokers are deeply curious, genuine, and compassionate. When they enter a community, it's not to exploit the community's assets but rather to grow and nourish them.

Being a broker is not easy work and it's not for everyone. Brokers bring vision, not agendas. They embrace vulnerability. They can acclimate to rejection, to the messiness of interactions and relationships, to uncertainty and ambiguity. They are gifted at catalyzing successful interactions and then fading away. And while they are people-oriented and intuitive, they are also rigorous and reflective, eschewing simplistic principles, platitudes, and techniques for a deeper understanding of the work.

Our role is to stretch beyond giving help and instead connect people with a life outside of programs and services—with meaningful jobs, friends, activities, and places where they experience belonging.

Stretch questions

- When does satisfaction with services signal a good outcome, and when does it signal a poor one because it has emphasized comfort and help over growth and change?

- Who makes a terrific broker? What experiences best prepare people for that role?

- How might infrastructure need to change (oversight, policies, training, etc.) to make it possible to recruit and support brokers?

6   Experts ⟳ Community Catalysts

JOE ERPENBECK, FACULTY member with the Asset-Based Community Development Institute in Chicago and experienced community developer, tells a story about a young woman with an intellectual disability who wanted to learn how to knit. Rather than register her in a workshop or link her up with some knitters, her support worker posted a notice in a local café: "Knitting Club on Wednesday nights, 7 to 9 p.m." On the first night, a handful of people showed up. Over the following weeks, the group continued to grow until it had almost fifty regular attendees and needed to find a new café.

What was especially beautiful about the knitting club were the bonds and connections that formed. The participants discussed their lives and their challenges. They shared wisdom and laughed together. The young woman with a disability was able to talk about her boyfriend and about the supervisor at work with whom she was struggling. The others listened and offered up advice. The woman's support worker had effectively created a new community from scratch, expanding the matting of connectivity rather than trying to stitch the woman in somewhere.

Sadly, before long, the disability community caught wind of this hospitable and inclusive setting and began showing up in droves. Vans would appear and people with disabilities and their staff would climb out and join the group. It changed things. The meet-up began to resemble a program site for disability services rather than a neighbourhood knitting club, and eventually the group unravelled.

AS THE SOCIAL services mature, and as funding and accountability flows develop, so do post-secondary programs and professional training. Every role in a social service organization comes with educational requirements and a training regimen. It's a sectoral norm, a requirement of accrediting bodies, a legislated responsibility, a risk mitigation strategy, and a quality improvement strategy. All stakeholders want well-trained, well-qualified staff, including the staff themselves.

Yet there are nowhere near enough staff or resources in the social service sectors to meet everyone's needs. Nor is it desirable to have social services meet everyone's needs, even if that were practicable. There's something to be said for people looking out for, and looking after, each other. Why have we eschewed that idea?

The health of a community should not be measured by the volume of available services, which is too often the indicator used, but by the community's level of interconnection and its ability to self-mobilize to advance individual and collective well-being. There is a lot of goodwill and capacity in a community—neighbours, businesses, places of worship, community groups, and so on. How do we better support and activate community networks?

Our modern experience with service technologies tells us that it is difficult to recapture professionally occupied space.

JOHN MCKNIGHT

When we Canadians asked our government, decades ago, to ensure that our vulnerable were looked after, we weren't suddenly relieved of our personal duties to them or to others around us. It's not up to government and social services to become the proxies for care in our society. The more we expect that, the more we impoverish our democracy (which is premised on civic engagement), as well as our resilience as communities and ourselves.

One unfortunate side effect of the professional training and designations in our sector is that they make community members feel they're not "qualified" to interact with the populations we support. They don't want to say or do the wrong thing, so they're reluctant to interact at all. For professionals, there's less tolerance of error because we are supposed to know what to say (or not) or do (or not). But when people encounter others as people, not as trained professionals, there's usually an abundance of tolerance, a willingness to connect, a shared curiosity and openness. Experts are expected to be experts; everyday people are not. Generally, they're expected only to be civil, to make an effort, to be real, to care.

As social service organizations, we need to get better at being part of community and contributing to its well-being. Too often we're in the position of asking for something or expecting something. How do we instead stretch our attention to notice what the community needs and offer our help and resources—not because we want something in return, or because we have an agenda in mind, but because investing in the vibrancy of neighbourhoods is what good neighbours do? Connection elevates everyone. We believe that in serving the common good, we will serve our own social missions in deeper, more enduring ways than through the delivery of programs and services.

Stretching our roles to become community catalysts involves more than asking people to volunteer for us or give donations or improve accessibility. Those approaches suggest that *we* are the solution, or are in possession of it. We aren't. What's more, conventional volunteering, though much vaunted, is an example of how formal systems can colonize the informal offerings of communities. Volunteering has become a quasi-professional occupation, with its own background checks, training, performance feedback, and monitoring. Too often it focuses on plugging people into our own systems and frameworks rather than activating all the ways people can make a difference. Volunteering takes the broad offer of community ("How can I help?" "How can I make a difference?") and converts it into units of unpaid labour, discreetly bound, subject to our policies, and channelled to meet our needs.

What if we simply invited and emboldened citizens to address shared objectives, things like caring and connected neighbourhoods, safe communities, personal fulfillment, social inclusion, diversity? What if we stopped applying the word "volunteer" to occasions of unpaid friendship or care and recognized them as ungovernable moments of human connection?

The malaise of social isolation is not a disability problem or a refugee problem or a seniors problem. It is a "we" problem, a community problem. What does belonging mean to all of us? What sort of neighbourhood do we want to live in? The answers to these and other questions cannot be theoretical; they must be enacted. Social service agencies cannot force an answer, nor can government. But we can ask the questions and convene people to answer them. And when people choose to cooperate to solve a shared problem or realize a joint opportunity, we can figure out how to support and enable them rather than pointing them to our own programs and services. We can also forge new hubs of connectivity (like knitting clubs and other meetups) rather than relying on existing ones. Instead of spending our time looking for hospitable places, we can create them—for everyone.

Community catalysts see the potential for connections and contributions in everyday people, places, and associations. They are alchemists who can convert that potential into reality. They are living flames, lighting up people's desire to connect and be part of something. They inspire people and are talented conveners. They have the gift of inviting and nudging, suggesting and asking. Only in the rarest circumstances might they impose on others or pluck the strings of obligation, though they are wise enough to know when that is what's needed to release the capacity within community.

Stretch questions

- How do we invite neighbours into conversations about a shared place and enable them to become the true creators and owners of interdependence, reciprocity, and mutual care?

- How can our organizations invest in neighbourhood connectivity, vibrancy, safety, and resilience?

- How can our organizations catalyze the informal capacities of communities so that neighbours are encircled by neighbours and blanketed by natural filaments of care?

7   Teachers ⟳ Coaches

GEORGE SAT AT the bar and smiled at the woman to his right. He wasn't sure what to say next, so he turned to his left and asked his coach for the night, Jesper, for advice. By the end of the evening George was revelling in a series of firsts: first personal conversation with a woman, first time on the dance floor, first time at a bar on a Saturday night.

George and his coach were at the bar as part of an experiment called Coach in Your Corner, one of the prototypes that emerged from our research months in Burnaby, living alongside adults with developmental disabilities. George lived on his own in the housing complex but didn't want to be alone. He wanted a girlfriend and eventually to get married. But he wasn't sure what to do. His psychiatrist and life skills worker offered strategies, but always in the abstract, never in context.

Coach in Your Corner was designed to fill the gap. The idea was to provide people with real-time, in-context feedback on relationships and dating. Developing meaningful relationships wasn't just a matter of learning interpersonal skills with a life skills worker or unpacking underlying issues with a therapist. It was about getting mentorship in the places where dates might unfold. George was good at starting conversations but wasn't always sure how to end them. From his coach, he got concrete suggestions and lots of encouragement.

To be who you are and become
what you are capable of is the only
goal worth living.

ALVIN AILEY

AFTER CAREGIVING, MOST interactions between employees and people with intellectual disabilities are likely to involve teaching. We teach every imaginable skill—hygiene, cooking, cleaning, laundry, financial literacy, paying bills, taking transit, setting dinner tables, saying "please" and "thank you," attending to personal space, and so on. We break complex tasks down into simpler ones. We create measurable goals. We build lengthy assessments and corresponding curricula. And we teach.

Sometimes, if we're honest with ourselves, what we do is less about teaching and more about preaching. Sometimes we try to point out the right or wrong way to do things. We try to impress upon people their need to behave in certain ways or to stop behaving in other ways, but we don't always follow through and actually teach anything. Instead of any particular pedagogy or art, we use personal homilies and exhortation. There is a tacit presumption that we are "smarter, wiser, and healthier" at this life stuff, and that our support role requires us to be regular advisors and sermonizers. But generally, beyond being helpers:helpees, we are teachers:students.

From a teaching perspective, we have learned that people with intellectual disabilities do much better in in situ than in theoretical settings. We've especially noticed this when it comes to employment. Employment readiness programs—programs that teach workplace skills (everything from hygiene to hierarchy)—have faced vociferous criticism because no matter how many months or years participants spend in these programs, they are rarely deemed ready to move on to employment. This is partly because there are things you can't get from a class, even if it offers snazzy videos, employer presentations, and workplace visits. This is especially true for concrete learners. Every context is nuanced, involving different physical environments, routines, expectations, personalities, and communication styles. People with disabilities best learn and adapt to specific contexts, rather than learning general skills and concepts and having to apply them to new settings.

Meanwhile, the mainstream world has discovered that books, therapists, and workshops are often not enough to help people navigate the messiness of life and make the changes they want to make. Too often people are enslaved to perspectives, impressions, and behaviours that lock them into the same historic patterns. They need guides, mentors, or coaches on the ground to help them shake free. Executive coaches emerged to empower leaders in areas ranging from time management to presentation skills to styles of communication and leadership. Life coaches began helping people become unstuck and realize their goals. Suddenly, instead of just telling people what to do and how to do it, teaching others was about sharing-with and doing-with.

Good coaches are like teachers in that they have tool sets, but they're not just teachers. And although they listen, validate, prompt, and encourage, they're not exactly therapists either. They bring conceptual frameworks to what they do, but they also bring intuition, creativity, and vibrancy. Coaches do more than teach or validate—they inspire. They stir motivation while dismantling stoppages caused by fear, anxiety, and low self-esteem. They empower people to take the steps in the world that they want to take but for whatever reason haven't. For us, coaching also means revealing structural impediments to personal power, and walking alongside people as they explore and exercise agency, confront stigma, and claim their place in the world.

Coaches build competence in particular areas of interest while at the same time applying themselves to the masonry of character: courage, discipline, perseverance, resolve.

In the social services, we should stretch beyond teaching the people we support and start coaching them. We should also consider how to coach circles, in particular family members. Although workshops and professional consultants have their place, the complexity of everyday family circumstances can be overwhelming to sort through without guidance. Parents often find themselves inhabiting roles they don't want to inhabit and stuck in patterns they don't want to be stuck in. Their well-being is not merely an instrumental consideration for achieving greater outcomes; it is its own end.

Stretch questions

- How do we strike the right balance between coaching frameworks, technique, and intuition?

- Is coaching a distinct role, or is it part of everyone's role?

- How do we coach circle members to go from roles such as master coordinator, nagger, or advocate, which they usually find exhausting and unsatisfying, to cheerleader, confidant, or ally?

14

Stretching our frameworks

THE SOCIAL SERVICES consist of, and are sustained by, an end-less series of frameworks, ranging from governance structures and labour agreements to philosophical commitments and strategic plans. These are the bases from which our cultures and practices emanate. The different frameworks are machined to fit together as best as possible, though there is always abrasion.

Here, we propose stretching five frameworks that underpin the social services. In rethinking and augmenting these dispositions, we hope to make room for new approaches to what we do, and for new ways of working and being.

8 Triage ☼ Prevention

KAREN, WHO HAD no formal affiliation with any organization, was invited to speak to leaders of several community organizations. She told them that when she moved to her neighbourhood eight years earlier, she decided it was time to live her convictions.

Karen opened her house to students and young people in transition, many of whom were struggling to find their place in the world and needed someone to talk to and guide them. Meal times now consisted of several people preparing and eating together. Then she began hosting a quarterly soup dinner for neighbours, no RSVP required. Soon there were forty to fifty neighbours showing up. Before long, regular musical performances started up, along with a neighbourhood Easter egg hunt, a community garden, and other activities. Neighbours began connecting on their own and exchanging keys.

The cohesion that developed between neighbours had a spillover effect. When the Syrian refugee crisis occurred, the neighbourhood sponsored a Syrian family who moved into a resident's basement suite. The new family was quickly folded into the area's social fabric and rhythms, and they reciprocated by offering a class on Syrian cuisine. The following year the neighbourhood sponsored a second family.

Karen also told the organizational leaders that she was thinking about what would happen to her when she got older. She imagined she would find a solution with neighbours so that she wouldn't have to go into a long-term care facility or a seniors' residence. She had begun to work on transforming the roommate model into a

It is well known that "problem
avoidance" is an important part of
problem solving. Instead of solving
the problem you go upstream and
alter the system so that the problem
does not occur in the first place.

EDWARD DE BONO

committed community with long-term roommates, and on nurturing
friendships within the neighbourhood so that they functioned like
an extended family.

JUST AS HEALTH services provide medical triage to those in urgent
need, the social service sector provides a kind of social triage to people who face mental health challenges, addiction, homelessness,
poverty, and more. But in health services, there is also an investment
in prevention strategies. After all, it's better to not need hospitaliza-
tion than to receive good treatment while you're there. What is the
equivalent in the social service sector?

There is an abundance of compelling research that illustrates how
social connections and loneliness impact health outcomes (mortal-
ity rates, cancer, heart disease, addictions), mental health outcomes
(depression, anxiety, stress), education outcomes, crime rates, and

more. The greater your sense of belonging and social inclusion, the better you do—especially in emergencies. Growing and thickening the ties of social connection, as Karen helped to do in her neighbourhood, will make a difference in all sectors. Belonging isn't a fluffy concept or platitude; it's the stuff of life and death.

Only in more recent years has the public sector begun to recognize the preventative value of social ties. Even so, many still feel that the exclusive focus of our work is the people we identify as the recipients of our charity. They feel it would be unethical for us to use our limited resources to benefit anyone else. That sentiment was clearly expressed by a leader of a community-based organization sitting at the same table as Karen, who declared, "I am not supportive of promoting social connectivity for someone who drives a Mercedes in Shaughnessy. That person is not my concern. I am only interested in social inclusion for vulnerable people."

We would argue that this view is based on an unsophisticated charity model, one that's comfortable dividing the world into the haves and the have-nots, the doing-just-fine and the vulnerable, and one that sees individuals as the unit of intervention. It's not so simple. If the goal is to fold people into community life, what do we do when there is little sense of community? If the goal is belonging, what do we do when there is a hardly discernible web of connectivity? In such cases, no one is included in anything, no matter what their label. If we want inclusion in neighbourhoods and communities where "everyone else" lives—not just pockets for people with disabilities, or immigrants and refugees, or seniors—then we need to attend to both sides of the equation.

Shifting sociocultural norms so that we normalize caring, diversity, and personal accountability is a powerful way of moving upstream. Other upstream strategies could include addressing economic forces and dynamics and investing in the capacity and resilience of children, youth, and families. Social problems are complex. There will be no simple cause behind them nor any panacea to remedy them. We need many strategies and interventions, and we need creative people to conceive of them, and we need makers and tacticians to pursue them.

There is always pressure to spend money on the urgent needs we face every day, on direct services to those with disabilities or other groups. But we must stretch our investments to encompass preventative measures that will reduce the demand for social services in the first place. After all, these services are poor surrogates for a life well lived in community.

Stretch questions

- How do we repurpose organizational resources and roles so that we increase social connectedness, belonging, and resilience?

- What conditions can we create, or contribute to, that enable more community-minded people to come forward?

- What social norms, virtues, and competencies will lead to better starts, trajectories, and ends for all of us? How do we cultivate them?

9   Workers ⟳ People

JEN LOVED A good margarita by the pool in the company of good friends. Marjorie and Eloise fit the bill. They gossiped and planned wild vacations that, while unlikely to unfold as imagined, were a source of deep belly laughs.

As they lounged poolside, little separated Jen from Marjorie and Eloise. But on Mondays, all that changed. Jen's role shifted from friend to personal support worker, and Marjorie and Eloise's role shifted from friend to person served. At work Jen pretended she didn't know her friends' crushes and secrets. She tried to be professional. She did what her supervisors asked of her, and not much more. She ended her days writing log notes and revealing as little information as possible. "They don't need to know much," Jen said, referring to the system. "What are they going to do with it anyway? Get me in trouble?"

Jen's weekday circumspection contrasted with her weekend care-freeness. The service system, she thought, demanded that she be friendly but distant, responsible and cautious, and definitely not too much fun.

Jen, Marjorie, and Eloise inhabited two contradictory worlds, one that felt authentic and natural, and another that felt obligatory and bounded. Had the system, in its quest for standardization, fairness, and clarity, squeezed out too much personality, zest, and colour?

WE RECALL AN organizational leader once declaring, "Clients will always come first, but employees are a close second." We understood the sentiment, which was intended to be an affirmation of employees, but it didn't sit well. Did it need to be set up as a competition?

The reason our services exist is to serve people with disabilities and their families. Our workers are absolutely essential to that—they are the ones in direct relationships with people. But too often our sector's prevailing view of workers is one of instrumentality. Employees are seen as an important means to an end, but not as an end themselves. At least, not so far as organizations are concerned. Not on the worksite. To even contemplate workers as ends in and of themselves would put their needs and interests in competition with those who access our services.

There is without question a lot of investment in the employer-employee relationship, because that relationship determines whether there's enough trust, consensus, resources, and training for the agency to fulfill its contractual commitments. And there are countless

In organizations, real power and energy is generated through relationships. The patterns of relationships and the capacities to form them are more important than tasks, functions, roles, and positions.

MARGARET J. WHEATLEY

mechanisms in place to make sure that fulfillment happens—collective agreements, performance management and training systems, disability management, wellness initiatives, employee recognition, complaint processes, whistle-blowing policies, and more. All of these formal undertakings are meant to foster a healthy, functioning workforce. But are today's employer-employee relationships conducive to the work and life we envision for the future? Perhaps it's time to stretch the labour framework and reconstruct the role of workers, the obligations of organizations, and the relationship between the two.

Labour relations are usually characterized by transactional, rule-based features that, underneath, view employees as somewhat reluctant instruments in the hands of somewhat incompetent or capricious leaders. Trust can be fickle and easily eroded, and suspicion and wariness may persist even in the face of goodwill. This legacy, founded on mistrust, provides unsatisfactory grounds for rehumanizing our work.

What if we could find a deeper premise to the worker-employer relationship? Our contractual and professional obligations do not, after all, determine our moral ones. An ethical disposition that sees people as ends cannot be selectively applied to one group of people (those served) and not another (those who serve). The duty to others cannot be disaggregated—otherwise, we are not being serious.

What would happen if we broadened our vision of flourishing to include workers among the people who should flourish? What if we pursued vibrancy and connection in work environments just as we pursue them in neighbourhoods and communities?

It is past time to question the boundaries that circumscribe our relationships to one another, as professionals, and to the people we serve. There are doubtless good reasons why these boundaries were created, including concerns about fairness, clarity, consistency, wellness, and vulnerability. But have we so cluttered the relational space with rules and roles that we've made it impossible to be present? And if we can't be present, if we can't have authentic personal exchanges with the people we support and with one another, if we can't be vulnerable or express the pulse of our heart or the tug of personal duty, how much of what we make becomes artifice? How much do we press relationships into the mould of technician:object or helper:helpee? How much do we become manufacturers of care, of pretense? Why can't we take our place in relationships as whole people rather than just as workers?

As we've said earlier, the needs of systems and humans don't often align, which makes this stretch particularly challenging. But the foundation of our work—and of life—is personal and relational. When we lose that foundation, we lose our compass, our legitimacy, ourselves.

Stretch questions

- We may need rules and agreements for employees, but can we nest them in a deeper, more inspiring framework of care and relatedness?

- Can we evolve the employer-employee relationship so that the goal is not just to establish respectful and functional work environments but also thriving ones where workers, too, can flourish? Where meaning, joy, beauty, and growth freely abound?

- How do we neutralize corrosive conceptions of labour that downplay employees' dedication, hard work, long hours, and often willing sacrifices around wages, time, and family, and that regard workers as burdensome cost centres that draw resources away from those who really need them?

10   Programs ⟳ Platforms

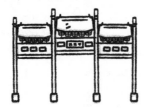

AMIN KNEW A lot about chickens. Growing up in Iran, he took care of his family's animals as well as his neighbour's. When his family immigrated to Canada, he lost his connection to place and to people. He found himself staying inside most days, feeling listless and depressed. Speaking English wasn't easy. Meeting people was even harder.

We have to restore power to the family, to the neighborhood, and the community with a non-market principle, a principle of equality... of let's-take-care-of-one-another. That's the creative challenge.

JERRY BROWN

That's where Amin's community connector came in, helping introduce him to new people, new places—and a new platform. Kudoz, the prototype we developed to connect people with and without disabilities to broad-ranging experiences, sparked Amin's curiosity. He tried landscape photography, learned how to set up recycling systems, and discovered the history of his city's Chinatown. He even went burlesque dancing for the first time.

Not only did these new experiences help Amin practice his English, they also gave him and his family fresh subjects to talk about and reflect on. Amin's sister, seeing his newfound interest in dance, discovered a dance course for him at the local community centre. The Kudoz platform did more than connect Amin to experiences. It deepened his connections to his family and helped expand his independence and opportunities.

WHEN WE SAY "platforms" we may sound like we're talking about technological solutions. We're not. We're talking about the way services are designed and delivered, no matter what kind of technology is (or isn't) involved.

Our social service system is built around programs. There are many of them, and for good reason—they've played or continue to play important roles. They provide stability, skill development, and care. Programs, however, are not always people-centred. They tend to be highly structured, involving eligibility criteria, referral and assessment protocols, scheduled hours and activities, policies, and much more. They also tend to have high caseloads. These factors make it difficult to meaningfully accommodate individual circumstances or differences, and some individuals are not accommodated at all.

Moreover, program accountability is not, first and foremost, to the recipients. The organization that delivers a program is responsible to funders and stakeholders for the results. There are internal and external reporting requirements around participant attendance, progress, and conduct. A "client-driven" or "family-driven" service is only notionally so, despite the ready propagation of such rhetoric.

A platform is different. It connects people rather than delivering a service. It's the difference between a hotel (program) and Airbnb (platform), or a taxi service and Uber. A platform is a way of bringing people together around a common set of needs, opportunities, or values. It's a way for people to share resources and passions, to exchange solutions to mutual problems, and to meet others. A platform grows and leverages the power of informal networks, whereas a service provides specialized support and programming within specific parameters.

A platform is a tool that people can make use of—or not. Both the use and the results are up to the individual. People use a platform to advance their own needs or interests, at their own pace, and in accordance with their own desired outcomes. And they do this with everyday people in the community, rather than by attending a program that is delivered by professionals and that is ultimately "owned" by organizations and funders.

For the social services, stretching beyond a model of service delivery to one of embracing platforms is like going from running a construction company to organizing a barn-raising. Platforms mobilize citizens. They facilitate connections and engagement between people, families, neighbourhoods, and communities—connections that are the lifeblood of the new focuses and roles we envision for our sector in the future. Platforms can be customized to respond to contemporary issues, and they engender self-determination and cooperation. They magnify the power of everyone's creativity and cooperation.

This is not an easy stretch. There's a strong tendency in our sector to turn everything into a program—to assign a manager, put together a plan, recruit people to be part of it, determine joint activities, find resources. The new idea quickly becomes just another pilot program or project controlled from the top down. Stretching toward a platform requires that organizations cede control. It means becoming excellent conveners and enablers, and that is all. If we want more solutions, more community connection and cooperation, and more self-determination for those we support, we need to learn how to bring people together and how to stay out of their way.

Stretch questions

- How can we build more platforms that connect diverse people, that offer useful tools to help people live better lives, and that can bring people and community members together to realize opportunities and create their own solutions?

- How do we supply the right environments and resources to enable people to capitalize on the wisdom and creativity that occurs when people gather, rather than continuing to be the source of solutions and the deliverers of programs?

- How do we learn to nourish and resource the new solutions that emerge when people meet?

11 Delivery ⟳ Development

BELLA WAS A "Jane of all trades," a talented guitarist and singer, a poet, an artist, and a support worker for a disability organization. She worked one-on-one with an older woman with a disability. They had an easy rapport and knew each other so well they could practically read each other's minds. But increasingly, Bella felt out of ideas for what they could do together. They had gone to all the parks, museums, and community centres. She wondered what else was out there.

Where teachers might have time to plan their lessons each week, Bella did not. The thirty hours a week she worked were busy. She barely had time to write her log notes at the end of the day. Nor was Bella's role ever contextualized to be about learning and development. She didn't have much access to the latest research or thinking. Every year she got recertified in familiar areas like first aid/CPR, food safety, and providing behavioural support, but she didn't learn anything new.

Nothing changed until Bella became part of a research and development team coached by InWithForward. Suddenly she was dedicating a week a month to generating and testing fresh ideas for the disability sector: some that might directly benefit the woman she supported, and some that might reinvigorate the staff culture.

But Bella's involvement was an extra cost that her agency needed to cover, and they couldn't keep it up indefinitely. Besides, most months Bella's manager couldn't spare her because there weren't enough casual workers to replace her. It was all too easy for the status quo to continue.

The greatest danger in times of turbulence is not the turbulence; it is to act with yesterday's logic.

PETER DRUCKER

THE SOCIAL SERVICE sector is designed to deliver services. All of our departments, roles, and resources are pointed at doing that well. High-quality delivery matters, but without a rigorous development side, the programs and services we provide can become static, irrelevant, and over-sustained. They can make situations worse. There are too many instances of people who experience developmental and intellectual regression, social isolation, disempowerment, system dependency, and diminished resilience because the services they receive don't properly align with their needs. Without research and development, we tend to do the same things over and over, with only minor adjustments. Not much will change.

R&D is not the same thing as setting up new projects or pilot programs, even when they're called innovative and creative. The approach in such cases is too often based on "more of the same." The problem is already assumed (for example, lack of skills, lack of employment), the desired outcome is established, basic assumptions and values are left buried and unchallenged, data is drawn from traditional sources (such as surveys and focus groups), and the solution is invented, developed, and implemented by senior professionals who are steeped in the current paradigm.

True development begins with questions, not solutions. It begins with rigorous inquiry—investigating problems from multiple perspectives, looking at different kinds of data, excavating historical and contemporary values and assumptions, involving users in defining and co-creating solutions, prototyping new practices. It involves completely new roles, competencies, data, evaluation frameworks, methods, and relationships with those served.

Social R&D is much more than a specific project; it's a function that requires a long-term commitment of resources. It is incredibly difficult to do within bureaucracies and systems because it involves stretching from a culture of delivery, which is heavily accented with accountability and compliance, to a culture of inquiry, creativity, and experimentation.

Without true development, our systems will continue to give birth to pilots that bear the same genetic profile of the current system, and they will grow up to become programs that resemble what we already have. Our quality improvement loops and strategic planning processes are inadequate substitutes. These self-validating exercises simply consolidate our existing practices and systems by endlessly refining them—they improve what already exists rather than supplying us with next practices. ("Moving from best practice to next practice" was a phrase coined by Maggie Vilvang, relationship manager with Grounded Space.) Processes like these extend the life cycle of current services and organizations; they don't disrupt them.

The imperative to get better at what we do must be complemented by an imperative to generate new and disruptive approaches to our work. And we need a standard to distinguish between incremental improvement to existing practice and new, disruptive approaches.

Stretch questions

- How do we create social R&D infrastructure that serves as an engine for continuously producing new solutions?

- Whom do we need to convince that social R&D is essential? With whom do we need to partner?

- Where do we situate a social R&D function so that it's close enough to organizations or "the ground" to ensure there is take-up, but not so close that institutional needs and cultures smother the process?

12   Rights ⟳ Culture

AT A PALLIATIVE care roundtable in Ottawa, a rich discussion ensued about how our western culture is unprepared for death. People want to die well but may not know what that means. There isn't much public investment in death. The health services focus on restoring health and extending life, not supplying good deaths, and the public seems unaware of how to prepare for the end of life. It's a future problem that most of us put off until it's too late.

Dominator culture has tried to keep us all afraid, to make us choose safety instead of risk, sameness instead of diversity. Moving through that fear, finding out what connects us, reveling in our differences; this is the process that brings us closer, that gives us a world of shared values, of meaningful community.

bell hooks

The group wrestled with how to boost awareness. How could they convince governments to spend more on palliative, end-of-life care? How could they share research and create a call to action? What legal, political, and educational strategies could they invoke?

Al Etmanski spoke to the challenge eloquently. "Cultural receptivity precedes political receptivity," he said. That is, instead of thinking about how to compel politicians to act the way you think they should, first consider how to shift social norms. Invite performance artists, musicians, and storytellers to explore the topic of good deaths. Find ways to make death part of our media feeds so that the subject spills over into our everyday conversations. If good lives and good deaths were what we talked about, there would be no need to convince politicians of anything, and any measures that got enacted would be less vulnerable to the vagaries of political interest.

IN THE DISABILITY sector individuals, families, and organizations have fought hard for more inclusive and accessible education, services, cities, and institutions. It has been a hard fight and we're still not there.

Along the way we have tended to promote change by focusing on political and educational remedies rather than the cultural currents that convey us. We've looked to political and statutory remedies as the primary mechanisms of change. Human rights legislation is a good example. Because legal entitlement—people's right to funding, services, accessible transportation and cities, economic participation, and workplace accommodations—is enforceable, it's a lever we frequently pull.

Yet there's a cost. Rights are about entitlement and enforcement, about power and contest, and while some may thrill in the fight, most are harmed by it. Stigma can be reinforced, "offenders" feel misunderstood and threatened, champions face burnout and ostracism. People go to their corners, they hyperbolize, and they either don't talk (and simmer) or they fight (and get hurt). Battles are sometimes necessary—without them we'd have no civil rights or deinstitutionalization—but there are other powerful tools beyond rights and advocacy, such as popular media. If only we knew better how to use them.

Consider television shows like *Will & Grace* and celebrities like Ellen DeGeneres. They did more than normalize the cultural legitimacy of the LGBTQ community—they popularized it. Gay culture and sensibilities became a topic of academic and popular enquiry, and of celebration. As the public began to see this community as culturally legitimate and an important part of the "story of us," a slew of political and legal barriers tipped over, paving the way for same-sex marriage, employment benefits, adoption, and other legal protections.

The stories we share, which feed into our collective sensemaking, are incredibly important. The stories tell us what's good and bad, healthy and sick, desirable and undesirable, safe and dangerous. If we change those stories, what stays the same?

It is a much more difficult proposition to impose a new story through an act of legislation or an educational video than it is to

If our culture and society aren't ready for change, new laws and policies will only produce social tension and be vulnerable to reversal.

sensitize people through arts, culture, and media. Movements are cultural revolutions owned by people, not organizations or institutions. They are the voices of tens of thousands and sometimes millions of people who share a conviction, a vision. They pour into the public square. When they rally, they can bring corporations and governments and the powerful to their knees. They are our peers, families, neighbours, celebrities, and heroes. They are not entities following institutional agendas; they are people envisioning a better story.

Especially now, when the rise of ultra-conservatism and populism around the world threatens to undo decades of work in social justice, multiculturalism, and diversity, our sector would do well to learn about movements. We need to understand how they form and drive change, to discover how to inspire and engage people at the grassroots level, and to find out how to tether our stories to the stories of pre-existing movements. If we want a new world for the people we serve, one where they are folded into society, we can't just shoehorn them in by means of legislation. We need to appeal to the public's imagination. We need to mobilize tools that activate empathy and understanding so that the collective sense of "we" naturally expands. If our culture and society aren't ready for change, new laws and policies will only produce social tension and be vulnerable to reversal.

How do we go about creating new stories? Charities are conditioned to tell *the* story—that is, to build a sense of urgency for funders or to validate impact through storytelling. Too often this *preserves* a dynamic of otherness rather than changing it. It's unlikely that public awareness campaigns, or even social innovation, will drive the deep culture change we are after.

The stuff of history—our conceptions of human existence and our recollections of who we were and who we became—is best told through the arts and humanities. Today we can add social and popular media to the tools at our disposal to stir the imagination and build a new story. Fifty years ago, radio, television, and newspapers pushed information to citizens. Today people generate their own content on YouTube and Instagram. They teach classes using platforms like Udemy and MasterClass. They share rides, homes, and experiences; review products and services; and interact with others around the world through an endless menu of games and apps. These whiplash developments have caught the social sector flat-footed. Instead of harnessing their power, we dip our toes in the water and use them as mere media channels to push our messages out.

Had people with intellectual disabilities been on our TVs and in our popular media in ways that celebrated their differences rather than stereotyping them, had they not been portrayed as creatures deserving of charity, or as special interest groups entitled to a piece of the pie, perhaps our gains would have been easier, quicker, and smoother. When people who are different from us are more visible, it's easier to have natural exchanges and interactions, which in turn dismantle stereotypes and otherness. Curiosity, empathy, generosity, and imitation are powerful impulses. When we make space in our imagination and hearts for people who are different from us, it is so much easier to make space for them in our stores, schools, and places of work.

Stretch questions

- How do we create stories that reflect the experiences and sensibilities of people living on the margins?

- How can we share these stories, vocabularies, and points of view so that they help shape broader social narratives—not as educational devices but as new cultural touchstones?

- What strategies do we need in order to intervene at deeper cultural levels? With whom do we need to partner—artists, art collectives, influencers in popular media, social media, and the humanities?

Conclusion

SYSTEMS BUILT FOR humans are not necessarily humane systems. They can be disempowering and humiliating. They can overlook lives instead of witnessing them. They can point out the parched spaces and ignore the verdant ones. While hope and healing lie in relationships, too often our human systems are cool, distant, and transactional. Murmurs of apology can be heard everywhere, admissions that these are just the rules and roles and hopefully others can appreciate that. Systems like that are hard on those who seek help, and hard on those who deliver it.

We have asked you, in this book, to consider a basic question about the social services: are we only safety nets, holding and protecting the people we support, or are we also trampolines, launching people into flourishing lives? If we want to be trampolines, then we need to stretch what we do, how we do it, and who we are. We need to accept the tensions that push and pull the social sector that we're part of and recover, in the spaces between, a place for soul.

We have a long road ahead of us.

The twelve stretches we're proposing may sound straightforward on paper, but they're not so straightforward in practice. We have to reimagine and tinker with so many components—procurement, evaluation, roles, competencies, training, resources, policies, practices. And people's expectations must change—about the role that services play, about what the system can or ought to provide.

We also need to rethink the values that underpin our work, and the assumptions and routines that currently inform what we do. Values, ideologies, and system imperatives must be made explicit and must be challenged if we are to loosen their tyrannous holds. The notions of risk and accountability must be deconstructed and reconstructed. Relationships with end users must change. How we show up in community must change.

The list is almost endless, and it may feel daunting to you. It feels daunting to us.

An important starting point is conversation. The sorts of things people talk about and think about is an important indicator of what they will do. If we want to imagine and perform something differently, key ingredients of our thinking must change. Our experiences must change. Our language too. Falling back on system language will only validate and consolidate what already exists. As tempting as it may be to imagine far-reaching legislation or new service models, the fact is that system change is more likely to come about through far more pedestrian means, like daily conversations and interactions. Exploring new ideas, talking about them, trying things a little differently—this is how we produce new possibilities, new rhythms, and in time, new cultures.

We should take heart that this is not a one-year, three-year, or even five-year undertaking that we propose; it's a project of a decade or two. It means committing our organizations to a journey that we may not be around to see through. But if the journey is worth it—and after years of seeing what doesn't work and of experimenting with what might, we believe it is—now is a good time to begin.

As we begin to stretch ourselves and our organizations, as we test our elasticity and our tolerance of tensions, we must never lose sight of what matters most: are we delivering on our promise of good lives for people? If we aren't, we need to be honest and acknowledge that. There is always work to be done. There's no shame in that.

So much depends upon our willingness to change. We hold in our hands, our human hands, the well-being of others—someone's child, sibling, parent. There can be no hiding behind our systems and professions. It's time to tear down that artificial curtain and face our personal, moral, and existential obligations. No matter what role we may play in the social services, those obligations are staggering to comprehend. If they do not bring us to our knees, perhaps we've forgotten how much influence we have on people's futures, how lasting are the imprints we leave on their lives, how the dances we involve them in shape their movements in the world.

Acknowledgements

W E WOULD LIKE to begin by thanking our editor, Frances Peck, for her clarity, patience, and encouragement. She has taught us so much about the art of writing.

Gord, Degrees of Change

This book would not be possible without a broad cadre of thinkers, doers, and imaginers, as well as the people in the system, and their families, who allowed us to hang out with them and who leaned into the prospect of building something new.

This book is the result of many conversations with many people. Most critical to the conversation have been, for me, my co-author, as well as a handful of leaders from community living organizations who have been probing the limits of the existing social service system and relentlessly pursuing design specifications for a new one: Fernando Coelho, Richard Faucher, Tanya Sather, and Christine Scott. This cohort has been put through the paces and has survived, not only because of their drive to see something new, but also thanks to tremendous internal support from boards, directors, managers, and front-line staff who see the value of this work and who have regularly supplied us with their time, resources, and insights. And patience.

I'd like to particularly thank my boss Fernando for giving me this role in the first place and for entrusting me to help navigate a future direction. You have been a rock in tempestuous seas, an enabler in times of restriction and restraint.

I think I speak for the Degrees of Change agencies in wanting to acknowledge Vinita Prasad, Tess Huntly, Gareth Williams, Heather Johnstone, Lisa Joy Trick, Janey Roh, John Woods, Brooke Oxley, and Peter Greenwood, all of whom have been tasked with not only researching and prototyping new practices, but also implementing them—which is a much harder thing to do. We are also incredibly grateful to the teams at Kudoz, Building Caring Communities, Real Talk, Meraki, Fifth Space, and Grounded Space, who have served as the tip of the spear in our innovation efforts and furnished much of our practical learning. Particularly, a big thank-you to Janey Roh who has been the steady hand on the tiller that has brought Kudoz from concept to scale. It has been an incredibly turbulent journey, and we are so grateful to her for sticking with us and bringing her vision, heart, and smarts to the work! Thank you, also, to John Woods and Kelsey Savage, whose curiosity, thoughtfulness, and passion for equity and sexual health made Real Talk what it is today, and to Elizabeth Boyd and Stephanie Koenig, two wonderful designers and souls who have continued to develop Meraki while also prototyping new roles and practices and pivoting previous ones. And, of course, none of this work could have unfolded were it not for the generosity of foundations such as the McConnell Foundation, the Conconi Family Foundation, and the Vancouver Foundation, and for the strategic funding and support from Community Living BC. Especially, thanks to Jack Styan, VP of strategic initiatives at Community Living BC, who not only first hired me into the community living sector almost thirty years ago, but who has also been central to our efforts to research, test, and operational-ize new methods and approaches within BC.

Degrees of Change and I are also grateful to Al Etmanski and Vickie Cammack, who have been our personal sherpas over the past twenty-five years or more. Not only have they been tilling the soil of innovation and movement-making in BC and Canada, they have also shown us extraordinary generosity and graciousness and have taught us the value of growing the tent and building relationships with others. It was their counsel to put a stake in the ground by means of just such a publication as this, and to declare the future we were imagining.

There are many people whose passion, inspiration, and thinking have informed my own. This includes the extraordinary people of Exeko, whose profound vision, depth of analysis, and critical practice have been a continuous source of inspiration to me. It also includes Joe Erpenbeck and Karen Reed, real champions of grassroots community development, who have shown us how soulful citizens can go about building more connected, inclusive, and resilient neighbourhoods.

The members of the InWithForward/Degrees of Change research team involved in the Burnaby Starter Project (Janey Roh, Laura Cuthbert, Sabrina Dominguez, Muryani, Jonas Piet, and Sarah Schulman) were the nexus of so much learning for us. This was one of the richest and most memorable experiences we have ever undertaken, and it signalled the start of an incredible journey. Thank you for that.

Lastly, I want to express deep gratitude to everyone who has been part of the InWithForward team. You have brought conceptual, ethical, and methodological rigour to our innovation efforts; supplied us with new vocabularies, research, and terms of reference; introduced us to your vast international networks of thinkers and doers; and reshaped our imagination and our expectations. This book would not exist were it not for the journey you have taken us on. It has changed us.

Sarah, InWithForward

The stories we tell here would not be possible without brave leadership. Our partnership with Gord Tulloch and the Degrees of Change agencies have been nothing short of transformative. We moved to Canada and have stayed in Canada because, despite some real frustrations and disappointments, we couldn't find better collaborators and co-conspirators. It's a beautiful thing to not feel alone. Tanya Sather and Richard Faucher at Burnaby Association for Community Inclusion, Christine Scott at Kinsight, and Fernando Coelho at posAbilities have put so much of themselves and their professional identities on the line to hold the space between old and new, structure and emergence, tradition and novelty.

Operating in the space between is both exhilarating and exhausting. This work isn't so much a job as a way of being. InWithForward only exists because we find extraordinary people who want to be with us, learn with us, scream with us, and grow with us. A mighty thank-you to the team who founded InWithForward: Jonas Piet and Muryani, two intrepid co-travellers who gave much of themselves to closing the gap between vision and practice. Over the past five years, we've been blessed with a growing team of designers, ethnographers, community mobilizers, and organizers. Daniela Kraemer, Natalie Napier, Maggie Vilvang, Jennifer Charlesworth, Valentina Branada, Anna Bond, Jess Jamieson, Melanie Camman, Clarence Tam, and our many former team members and fellows are each a part of the InWithForward story.

Kudoz would not exist today without the incredible Janey Roh, and her team, who do the hard work of sustaining the space between delivery and development. Janey is a true friend, partner, and co-creator. She's in good company with John Woods and Kelsey Savage, who so thoughtfully lead Real Talk, along with the wonderful Elizabeth Boyd and Stephanie Koenig who steward Meraki. I have so much gratitude for our collective soul work: for embracing the hard questions, ethical quandaries, and imperfections in pursuit of trampolines.

Of course, our story would not be possible without the stories of hundreds of people who, by virtue of systemic injustices, are too often marginalized, sidelined, and silenced. These are people like Fay and Karen, who were our neighbours at the social housing building in Burnaby, our first home in Canada. We recognize the profound privileges we hold and the responsibility that comes with bearing witness to people's experiences, ideas, confusions, hopes, and challenges. We are at our best when we are deeply listening and humbly learning how to pay attention to the voices and wisdom of our fellow humans. May we muddle and stumble forward, together.

Plain language summary

WE THINK IT'S time for new roles and interactions, models, and policies. That means adjusting and adding to our current practices, along with coming up with new ideas, so that we can move toward more meaningful work and lives.

What is the point of our services?

1 It's not enough to keep people safe and help them get through their days. We also need to help people live full and happy lives.

2 Basic things like food, clothes, and a home are important, but so are beauty, purpose, and love. How do we work on those things too?

3 We spend a lot of time with people on activities, goals, and building skills. We need to spend more time finding out who they are and who they want to be in the world.

4 We need to get better at involving friends and family, because they are important. The more they believe in the possibilities of the people we support, the more the people we support are likely to succeed and live full lives.

What new roles do we need for workers?

5 Our staff are highly trained to help people, but that's not enough. We need to get better at supporting people to become part of community life.

6 Our cities and neighbourhoods are full of people who aren't trained in social services but have a lot to offer. We need to get better at helping everyone use their abilities and interests to make more caring, connected, happy communities.

7 We want people to become the best they can be in life. That means not only teaching them skills, but also inspiring and encouraging them.

How do organizations need to change?

8 A lot of the work that organizations do is to help people so that bad things don't happen to them or to others. We need to help. But we should also try to understand what causes people to break down or get in trouble or not be safe, and we should try to fix that.

9 Workers are people too. They aren't robots doing a job and getting paid. We need to find ways to let them be human at work.

10 Instead of our programs being the only answer to what people need, we should get better at connecting people in the community so that they can find their own answers together.

11 Organizations are usually good at providing programs and services. But they aren't very good at researching, coming up with, or testing new ideas. We need to learn how to do that or we'll be stuck with the same kinds of services forever.

12 We can't just rely on education and the law to break down barriers that keep people from living the best lives they can. We need to spend more time changing the way people think and feel about the people we support.

Stretch questions

Stretching our focuses

Stretch 1: Safety ⟲ Flourishing

- How do we rework accountability frameworks so that they're informed by deeper philosophical and psychological conceptions of human needs and striving?

- How do we use vulnerability as a force of social change rather than as a worrisome susceptibility that emphasizes that people are unsafe?

- How do we distribute risk so that it's shared, not only by employees, organizations, and governments, but also by individuals, circles, and communities?

Stretch 2: Body ⟲ Soul

- How do we address purpose and beauty through our work, and present opportunities to reflect on existence and the individual's place in it?

- How do we change our conversations so that they're not just about program curricula, activities, or goals, but also about the stuff of life? How might the two come closer together?

- How do we invite spirit or mana back into our institutions and create a protected place for it?

Stretch 3: Behaviour ⟲ Identity

- How has our involvement in the lives of those we support positively and negatively influenced their identities? What stories have they internalized?

- How do we introduce new scripts, language, and imagery that might enable people to adopt more constructive and healthier views of themselves and their place in the world?

- How do we address deep emotions like shame, helplessness, and inadequacy and cultivate new narratives to overcome them?

Stretch 4: Individuals ⟲ Circles

- How do we engage circles (family, friends, neighbours) without (further) disempowering individuals?

- Circle members face struggles in their own lives—how do we apply resources differently so that we can address everyone's wellness?

- How do we build the resilience of the entire network and not simply enlist their support?

Stretching our roles

Stretch 5: Helpers ⟲ Brokers

- When does satisfaction with services signal a good outcome, and when does it signal a poor one because it has emphasized comfort and help over growth and change?

- Who makes a terrific broker? What experiences best prepare people for that role?

- How might infrastructure need to change (oversight, policies, training, etc.) to make it possible to recruit and support brokers?

Stretch 6: Experts ⟳ Community Catalysts

- How do we invite neighbours into conversations about a shared place and enable them to become the true creators and owners of interdependence, reciprocity, and mutual care?

- How can our organizations invest in neighbourhood connectivity, vibrancy, safety, and resilience?

- How can our organizations catalyze the informal capacities of communities so that neighbours are encircled by neighbours and blanketed by natural filaments of care?

Stretch 7: Teachers ⟳ Coaches

- How do we strike the right balance between coaching frameworks, technique, and intuition?

- Is coaching a distinct role, or is it part of everyone's role?

- How do we coach circle members to go from roles such as master coordinator, nagger, or advocate, which they usually find exhausting and unsatisfying, to cheerleader, confidant, or ally?

Stretching our frameworks

Stretch 8: Triage ⟳ Prevention

- How do we repurpose organizational resources and roles so that we increase social connectedness, belonging, and resilience?

- What conditions can we create, or contribute to, that enable more community-minded people to come forward?

- What social norms, virtues, and competencies will lead to better starts, trajectories, and ends for all of us? How do we cultivate them?

Stretch 9: Workers ⟳ People

- We may need rules and agreements for employees, but can we nest them in a deeper, more inspiring framework of care and relatedness?

- Can we evolve the employer-employee relationship so that the goal is not just to establish respectful and functional work environments but also thriving ones where workers, too, can flourish? Where meaning, joy, beauty, and growth freely abound?

- How do we neutralize corrosive conceptions of labour that downplay employees' dedication, hard work, long hours, and often willing sacrifices around wages, time, and family, and that regard workers as burdensome cost centres that draw resources away from those who really need them?

Stretch 10: Programs ⟳ Platforms

- How can we build more platforms that connect diverse people, that offer useful tools to help people live better lives, and that can bring people and community members together to realize opportunities and create their own solutions?

- How do we supply the right environments and resources to enable people to capitalize on the wisdom and creativity that occurs when people gather, rather than continuing to be the source of solutions and the deliverers of programs?

- How do we learn to nourish and resource the new solutions that emerge when people meet?

Stretch 11: Delivery ⟳ Development

- How do we create social R&D infrastructure that serves as an engine for continuously producing new solutions?

- Whom do we need to convince that social R&D is essential? With whom do we need to partner?

- Where do we situate a social R&D function so that it's close enough to organizations or "the ground" to ensure there is take-up, but not so close that institutional needs and cultures smother the process?

Stretch 12: Rights ⟳ Culture

- How do we create stories that reflect the experiences and sensibilities of people living on the margins?

- How can we share these stories, vocabularies, and points of view so that they help shape broader social narratives—not as educational devices but as new cultural touchstones?

- What strategies do we need in order to intervene at deeper cultural levels? With whom do we need to partner—artists, art collectives, influencers in popular media, social media, and the humanities?

About the authors

GORD TULLOCH has worked in the developmental disability sector for almost thirty years. During this time, he served in many roles, from front-line worker to senior leadership, and as an accreditation surveyor, independent consultant, and college/university instructor. For the past several years he has worked as the director of innovation at posAbilities and focused on bringing in new methods, approaches, and partnerships that might produce meaningful and enduring system change. Gord holds a BA (Hons.) in philosophy and a master of arts in liberal studies. He hopes he can be a useful ally and co-conspirator to those calling for change.

DR. SARAH SCHULMAN has spent her career in buses, bingo halls, and back alleyways as a social scientist focused on the experiences of people living on the margins. She is a founding partner of InWithForward, an international social design organization whose teams have produced award-winning and scalable interventions. InWithForward is her fourth organization; she started her first in elementary school. Sarah holds a BA (Hons.) in human biology, a master's in education, and a DPhil in social policy from Oxford University, where she was a Rhodes Scholar. As a Jewish, middle-class, able-bodied, cisgender woman, Sarah is forever learning and un-learning how to show up and hold space for change.

Continue the conversation

REIMAGINING THE SOCIAL services and stretching our sector in new directions is an immense undertaking. It's also a collective one.

If you have ideas, experiences, successes, failures, or thoughts about the twelve stretches that you'd like to share, we would love to hear from you. You can check out some of the things we're up to at degreesofchange.ca, inwithforward.com, posabilities.ca, gord-tulloch .com, and trampoline-effect.ca. You can also reach out to us at gord@ trampoline-effect.ca or sarah@trampoline-effect.ca.